Schenker Salvi Weber

Vorwort

Seit 2009 sind die drei Architekten ein eingeschworenes Team. Sie sind in jungen Jahren aus unterschiedlichen Regionen nach Wien gezogen. Andres Schenker und Michael Salvi aus Bern, Thomas Weber aus Wangen im Allgäu. Und alle drei haben einen gemeinsamen Werdegang hinter sich. Über Lehren und anschliessende Hochschulen sind sie zum Architektenberuf gelangt. Dieser besondere Umstand mag auch ihre spezielle Neigung zur Architektur als einer Disziplin des «Machens» erklären, des Erschaffens eines Werkes aus den reellen technischen Möglichkeiten der Konstruktion und des Materials heraus. Das Wort «techne» bedeutete für Aristoteles die Verbindung der «schönen Künste» mit den Handwerkskünsten. Die Übereinstimmung des Umsetzens mit dem Erdenken. Das Erdenken findet jedoch jenseits von architektonischen Ideologien statt und konzentriert sich auf die «Sorgfalt und Genauigkeit des Machens» – wie es Dietmar Steiner in seinem aufschlussreichen Textbeitrag treffend benennt. So finden wir in diesem Band auch einige Modelle und Diagramme abgebildet, die das konkrete Herstellen erkunden, etwa das Diagramm zur Wohnbebauung Sillblock in Innsbruck, das darstellt, wie die wellenförmigen Balkonabfolgen sich um den parkartigen Hof schmiegen und daraus ein Konglomerat von verschachtelten Räumen resultiert, das spannende unorthodoxe Wohnungsgrundrisse mit vielfältigen Sicht- und Beziehungsachsen ermöglicht. Oder das detaillierte Fassadenmodell für die Post am Rochus in Wien, das die Schichtung und die Ausformulierung der Fassaden zeigt, die sich zu einer nuancenreichen, dichten architektonischen Wirkung entfaltet.

Es ist erfrischend, diese Studien zu verfolgen und dabei zu entdecken, wie die reelle Umsetzung handwerklich, materiell und konstruktiv perfekt gelingt, von einer besonderen Ausstrahlung von Präsenz und Solidität lebt und sich jeder formalistischen Neigung verweigert.

Heinz Wirz, Luzern im Juli 2018

Foreword

These three architects have been a close-knit team since 2009. They moved to Vienna from different regions at a young age. Andres Schenker and Michael Salvi are from Bern, while Thomas Weber comes from Wangen in the Allgäu region. All three can look back on similar careers so far. They came to the architectural profession via initial apprenticeships and subsequent university studies. That special circumstance may explain their specific tendency towards viewing architecture as a discipline of "doing", creating works out of the actual technical potential of construction and materials. Aristotle grasped the word "techne" as a combination of "fine arts" and the art of craftsmanship, therefore assuming a conformity between implementation and conception. That conception occurs outside architectural ideologies and focuses on the "care and precision of doing", as Dietmar Steiner succinctly states in his article. Thus, this volume presents a number of models and diagrams that investigate the concrete process of production. For instance the diagram for the Sillblock housing development in Innsbruck illustrates how the wave-shaped sequences of balconies wrap themselves around the park-like courtyard, creating a conglomerate of interwoven spaces that enables excitingly unorthodox apartment floor plans with diverse visual axes and interrelationships. Similarly, the detailed façade model for the Rochus post office in Vienna does not conceal the layering and formulation of the façades, which develop to create a dense architectural effect with diverse nuances.

It is refreshing to pursue these studies and discover how the actual implementation is achieved perfectly from the perspective of craftsmanship, materials and construction, thriving on the special radiance of presence and solidarity, while rejecting all formalistic tendencies.

Heinz Wirz, Lucerne, July 2018

16 De aedibus international

**Schenker Salvi Weber
Wien**

Quart Verlag Luzern

Schenker Salvi Weber
16. Band der Reihe De aedibus international / Volume 16 of the series De aedibus international

Herausgeber / Edited by: Heinz Wirz, Luzern
Konzept / Concept: Schenker Salvi Weber, Kristyna Trojanova, Wien AT; Heinz Wirz
Projektleitung / Project management: Quart Verlag, Antonia Wirz
Textbeitrag / Article by: Dietmar Steiner, Wien AT
Objekttexte / Project descriptions: Schenker Salvi Weber
Vorwort / Foreword: Heinz Wirz
Übersetzung Deutsch–Englisch / English translation: Benjamin Liebelt, Berlin DE
Textlektorat Deutsch / Text editing (German): Esther Pirchner, Innsbruck AT
Fotos / Photos: Bengt Stiller, Wien AT S. / p. 6, 10, 11, 14 (links / left), 20 (links / left), 21 (rechts / right), 34, 36, 38–45, 71 (rechts / right); Christoph Panzer, Wien AT S. / p. 12, 14–17, 19, 20 rechts / right), 21 (links / left), 66 (Bild / image 4); Lukas Schaller, Wien AT S. / p. 22, 26–33; Conné van d'Grachten, Ulm DE S. / p. 46, 48, 49; Peter Funke, Wien AT S. / p. 62, 65 (oben / top); David Meran, Wien AT S. / p. 65 (unten / bottom); Archiv Schenker Salvi Weber S. / p. 7–9, 24–25, 35, 51, 53, 54, 60 (unten / bottom), 63, 66 (Bild / image 2, 5), 68 (Bild / image 12), 69 (Bild / image 18), 70, 71 (links / left)
Modellbau / Model construction: Schenker Salvi Weber, Wien AT S. / p. 35, 53–54, 56–58, 60, 67 (Bild / image 7), 69 (Bild / image 18); Modellbauwerkstatt Gerhard Stocker, Wien AT S. / p. 24–25, 51, 63, 66 (Bild / image 2, 5)
Visualisierungen / Graphics: Kristyna Trojanova, Wien AT S. / p. 44, 47, 52, 56–58, 60; MISS 3, Brno CZ S. / p. 50, 66 (Bild / image 1), 67 (Bild / image 6, 9, 10), 68 (Bild / image 13), 69 (Bild / image 17); Schenker Salvi Weber, Wien AT S. / p. 67 (Bild / image 8); Janusch, Wien AT S. / p. 68 (Bild / image 11, 15), 69 (Bild / image 19); JAMJAM, Wien AT S. / p. 61; Ponnie Images, Köln DE S. / p. 68 (Bild / image 14); Klarbild Visuals, Bern CH S. / p. 66 (Bild / image 3), 69 (Bild / image 16)
Grafische Umsetzung / Graphic design: Quart Verlag, Antonia Wirz
Lithos: Printeria, Luzern CH
Druck / Printing: Printer Trento S.R.L., Trento I

© Copyright 2018
Quart Verlag Luzern, Heinz Wirz
Alle Rechte vorbehalten / All rights reserved
ISBN 978-3-03761-166-1

Quart Verlag GmbH
Denkmalstrasse 2, CH-6006 Luzern
books@quart.ch, www.quart.ch

6	Out of the box … ist das Motto / The motto is… Out of the box Dietmar Steiner
12	Wohnbebauung Sillblock, Innsbruck, Tirol / Sillblock housing development, Innsbruck, Tyrol
22	Post am Rochus, Wien / Post am Rochus, Vienna
36	Volksschule Absam Dorf, Absam, Tirol / Absam Village Primary School, Absam, Tyrol
46	Haus S, Ehingen, Baden-Württenberg / House S, Ehingen, Baden-Württemberg
50	Heime der Franziskanerinnen, Wien / "Heime der Franziskanerinnen" old people's home, Vienna
54	Volksschule Bütze, Wolfurt, Vorarlberg / Bütze Primary School, Wolfurt, Vorarlberg
58	Zinshaus Neutorgasse, Wien / Rented apartment building, Vienna
62	Teehaus, Wien / Tea house, Vienna
66	Werkverzeichnis / List of works
70	Biografie, Auszeichnungen, Ausstellungen, Vorträge, Bibliografie Biography, awards, exhibitions, lectures, bibliography

Out of the box ... ist das Motto

Dietmar Steiner

Was soll ich mit diesen jungen Architekten? Schenker Salvi Weber sind sympathisch und engagiert. Ihre Bauten und Projekte zeigen Intelligenz und eine besondere Qualität, die noch näher zu erläutern sein wird. Aber gibt es so etwas wie eine architektonische Position, eine Botschaft, eine Haltung in ihren Projekten, die mich interessieren sollte?

Dabei müssen wir mit den Produktionsbedingungen von Architektur beginnen, wie sie sich heute darstellen. Zunächst einmal ist es interessant, wie sich Architekturbüros heute organisieren, wie sie zusammenfinden. So hat sich auch die Bürogemeinschaft Schenker Salvi Weber anscheinend eher zufällig ergeben, durch Begegnungen und Freundschaften. Andres Schenker absolviert in Bern eine Zeichnerlehre, studiert an der Accademia di architettura in Mendrisio, wandert zu Zaha Hadid nach Wien und London. Michael Salvi, vier Jahre älter, absolviert ebenfalls in Bern eine Zeichnerlehre, dann die Fachhochschule Biel, und langsam verschlägt es ihn in renommierte Wiener Architekturbüros. Thomas Weber aber kommt aus dem Allgäu, macht eine Tischlerlehre, studiert an der Hochschule Biberach, arbeitet sich durch renommierte Architekturbüros der Region und landet in Wien. Es eint sie also eine mehr oder weniger alemannische Herkunft mit dieser ganzen Sorgfalt und Genauigkeit des «Machens» und sie finden zusammen in Wien, der mitteleuropäischen Hauptstadt der Schlamperei und des schönen Scheins. Alle drei sind also genealogisch und kulturell «fremd» in dieser Stadt und finden sich vielleicht gerade deshalb hier zusammen. Das ist ein Abbild der heutigen Situation der Architekturschaffenden.

Die nachwachsende Architektur Europas hat sich auch allgemein durch das sogenannte Erasmus-Phänomen (nach dem die kulturelle Mobilität fördernden europaweiten Stipendien-Programm) weitgehend egalisiert. Es spielt zwar immer noch eine Rolle, aus welcher lokalen Kultur man kommt, und die regionalen Produktions- und Rahmenbedingungen von Architektur sind immer noch stark unterschiedlich, aber die wandernden Identitäten amalgamieren in einem neuen Diskurs der Architektur, der jenseits konfligierender Positionen architektonischer Ideologien angesiedelt ist.

Ein kleiner kursorischer Rückblick sei mir deshalb erlaubt: Da waren zunächst die ideologischen Positionen der Nachkriegszeit. Modern gegen konservativ. Dann gab es die konsumistisch-kritischen und utopischen Träumereien, mit dem nun wiederentdeckten brutalistischen Mainstream im staatlichen oder kommunalen Auftrag. Dem folgte die

The motto is... Out of the box

Dietmar Steiner

What am I to do with these young architects? Schenker Salvi Weber are friendly and enthusiastic. Their buildings and projects express their intelligence and a special quality that will be explained below. But is there something like an architectural stance, a message, an attitude in their projects that I should be interested in?

Let us begin by looking at the production conditions that architecture faces today. It is interesting how architectural offices are nowadays organised and how they get together. It seems that the Schenker Salvi Weber partnership also joined forces more or less by chance, through encounters and friendships. Andres Schenker was a draughtsman's apprentice in Bern, studied at the Accademia di architettura in Mendrisio, before going to Zaha Hadid's offices in Vienna and London. Michael Salvi, who is four years older, was also a draughtsman's apprentice in Bern, before studying at the University of Applied Sciences in Biel and slowly establishing himself among renowned Viennese architectural offices. By contrast, Thomas Weber comes from the Allgäu region, was a carpenter's apprentice, studied at the Biberach University of Applied Sciences, worked his way through renowned architectural offices in the region and ended up in Vienna. What unifies them is their more or less German-speaking background and the great care and precision of craftsmanship. They came together in Vienna, the central European capital of sloppiness and beautiful superficial appearances. All three architects are genealogically and culturally "alien" in this city and perhaps that is the reason for coming together. It is a reflection of today's situation among architects.

The new generation of European architects is largely homogenised through the so-called Erasmus phenomenon (the European programme of grants that supports cultural mobility). One's specific cultural origins are still important; the regional conditions of production and underlying architectural situations still differ greatly, but the wandering identities amalgamate into a new architectural discourse that is situated outside the conflicting positions of architectural ideologies.

So allow me to present a cursory review: first, there were the ideological positions of the postwar years. Modern versus conservative. Then there were the consumer-critics and utopian dreamers, with a rediscovered Brutalist mainstream commissioned by the state or municipality. It was followed by the Postmodern return to the continuity of the European city. But some time in the latter decades of the last century, a new Modernism developed,

postmoderne Rückkehr zur Kontinuität der europäischen Stadt. Doch irgendwann in den letzten Jahrzehnten des letzten Jahrhunderts machte sich eine neue Moderne breit, man nannte sie die Zweite Moderne oder auch Revision der Moderne. Der Kontext der historischen europäischen Stadt wurde nun ignoriert. Die Zeile oder die verstreuten Objekte im grünen Niemandsland wurden wieder zum Modell. Städtebau als räumliche Organisation der Stadt wurde aufgegeben zugunsten isolierter Objekte im ignorierten Stadtraum. Das einzelne originelle Objekt, egal wo, egal wie, erhielt die mediale Aufmerksamkeit. Man nannte dies die Epoche der Stararchitekten.

In dieser Zeit hatte sich deshalb auch das Berufsbild des Architekten geändert. Bis in die 1980er-Jahre gab es noch die Unterscheidung in Business-Architekten und Kunst-Architekten. Die Kunst-Architekten hatten meist kleine Büros, die aber noch in der Lage waren, junge, unbedarfte Diplomanden nicht nur in den Ritualen des Gewerbes auszubilden, sondern auch einen inhaltlichen, innerarchitektonischen Diskurs zu entwickeln. Doch dies war diesen Architekten zunehmend ökonomisch nicht mehr möglich, weshalb sich junge Architekturschaffende zu Gruppen zusammenschlossen, um zunächst das gemeinsame Defizit erträglich zu halten.

Das künstlerische Einzelgenie ging weitgehend verloren, und damit auch die Signatur der unverkennbaren Autorschaft. Befördert wurde dieser Prozess durch die «digitale Technologie des Entwurfs», die zunehmend von den präfigurierten Standards der Software-Industrie gestaltet wurde. Damit ging auch die Autorschaft verloren, ein damals tragendes Element der Postmoderne. Jetzt fällt es natürlich schwer zu unterscheiden, was denn nun eine gute oder eine schlechte Architektur sei. Selbst das «Originelle» ist austauschbar geworden, immer perfekter camoufliert durch die autorenlosen Renderings.

In dieser von den Medien gehypten Ökonomie der Aufmerksamkeit sind also die Autoren und die Qualitäten der Architektur nicht mehr zu erkennen. Vielleicht sollten wir deshalb zurückkommen in die Wirklichkeit des Gebauten und wieder mehr vom Machen als vom Schein der Dinge reden. Schenker Salvi Weber helfen uns dabei. Alle drei kamen über die «Praxis» zur Architektur über Zeichner- und Tischlerlehre. Im Oktober 2009 verschränkten sich dann schicksalhaft die Lebensläufe der drei im inzwischen legendären Atelierhaus in der Wiener Schottenfeldgasse 72, einem versteckten, nicht besonders bedeutenden Industriebau im dicht verbauten, innerstädtischen 7. Bezirk

known as the Second Modernism or a "Revision of Modernism". It ignored the context of the European city. Once again, rows of buildings and scattered structures in green no-man's-land became the model. Urban planning, the spatial organisation of the city, was abandoned in favour of isolated objects in the ignored urban space. The individual original object, regardless where or how, was the focus of media attention. It was the age of the star architect.

During that period, the architect's professional profile also changed as a consequence. Until the 1980s, there was still a distinction between "business architects" and "art architects", the latter mainly having small offices that were nevertheless able to train young, inexperienced diploma students, not only in the rituals of the profession, but also in developing internal, content-based architectural discourse. But that became increasingly difficult for architects to fund, so young architects pooled their resources and formed groups, initially to make their common deficit tolerable. The artistic solo genius was lost and with it the signature of unmistakable authorship. The process was hastened by "digital design technology", which was increasingly shaped by the prefigured standards of the software industry. That put an end to authorship, which had once been a key aspect of Postmodernism. Today, it is naturally difficult to distinguish between good and bad architecture. Even "original" ideas have become interchangeable, since they are camouflaged by means of ever more perfect, authorless rendering.

Thus, in this media-hyped economy of awareness, the authors and qualities of architecture are no longer recognisable. So perhaps we should return to the reality of the built structures and speak more of doing than of the appearance of things. Schenker Salvi Weber help us in that respect. All three came to architecture via "practical experience" in draughtsman's and carpenter's apprenticeships. In October 2009, their three careers were interwoven as if by fate in the by now legendary studio building in Vienna's Schottenfeldgasse 72, a hidden, rather insignificant industrial building in the densely developed, inner-urban 7th district of Vienna. Its lofts are occupied by many young architectural offices, including caramel, urban architektur, Michael Wallraff, juri troy architects, feld72, Flatz Architektur, GABU Heindl Architektur and many others. The three exiles came together there and founded a joint office. The architects themselves confirm that the stable, triangular personnel structure is helpful, as is of course the opportunity to accommodate different capacity

in Wien. Dessen Lofts sind von vielen jungen Architekturbüros besiedelt, darunter caramel, urban architektur, Michael Wallraff, juri troy architects, feld72, Flatz Architektur, GABU Heindl Architektur und viele andere. Dort fanden sich die drei Exilanten zusammen und gründeten das gemeinsame Büro. Hilfreich sei die Struktur des personell stabilen Dreiecks, sagen die drei Architekten. Und natürlich auch die Möglichkeit, unterschiedliche Anforderungen der Kapazität in der «Szene» aufzufangen. Auch das befördert die inhaltliche Auseinandersetzung innerhalb der Generation.

Sie suchten dann gleich pragmatisch und professionell, in Wettbewerbe einzusteigen. Und anders als in früheren Jahrzehnten, als ein Oswald Mathias Ungers noch an 150 Wettbewerben erfolglos teilnehmen musste – wie er behauptete –, um den ersten zu gewinnen, gelang es ihnen bald, hier mit wichtigen Projekten zum Sieg und zur Realisierung zu gelangen. Interessant daran ist, dass sie nicht mit spektakulär plakativen Lösungen, sondern mit intelligenten Konzepten reüssieren konnten. So geschehen bei der Schule in Absam mit der Verlegung der Turnhalle unter die Erde und der damit eröffneten Möglichkeit, darüber einen attraktiven öffentlichen Raum für das Schul- und Dorfleben zu schaffen. So geschehen bei der heiklen Aufgabe des Dachausbaus der Cotton Residence, Wien. Derzeit werden in Wien sehr viele repräsentative Gründerzeitblocks der Ringstraßenzone zu luxuriösen Residenzen ausgebaut. Meist landen dabei befremdliche Ufos auf den historischen Dächern, die keinen Bezug zur bestehenden Struktur und Substanz aufweisen. Schenker Salvi Weber haben hier eine der besten und respektvollsten Lösungen entwickelt. Sie haben eine Sprache des «Weiterbauens» gewählt und gefunden, der man eine architektonische und ästhetische Nachhaltigkeit attestieren darf, die nach Jahrzehnten in die beruhigend schöne Wahrnehmung einer urbanen Selbstverständlichkeit kippen wird.

Schon darin drückt sich eine Haltung aus, die bei jeder Bauaufgabe sehr präzise die typologischen und morphologischen Parameter des Ortes analysiert. So geschehen auch bei den beiden wohl wichtigsten realisierten Projekten im bisherigen Schaffen von Schenker Salvi Weber, dem geförderten Wohnbau Sillblock in Innsbruck und der Post am Rochus in Wien.

Beim Sillblock ist es die Reaktion auf eine städtebauliche Situation, die eigentlich eine geschlossene Randbebauung zur Folge haben müsste. Schenker Salvi Weber teilen aber die Bebauung in zwei Winkel, eröffnen den Blick von der Strasse auf die vier geschützten Lindenbäume im gemeinschaft-

requirements "on the scene". That too encourages content-based discourse within the generation.

For pragmatic and professional reasons, they looked to enter competitions. Unlike earlier times, when for instance Oswald Mathias Ungers took part in 150 competitions – as he claimed – before winning the first one, they soon managed to succeed with important projects that were later erected. Interestingly, they thrived on intelligent concepts rather than spectacular, eye-catching solutions. For example, their design for the school in Absam sinks the sports hall underground, thereby creating an attractive public space for school and village life. It was a similar case with the difficult task of a roof extension for the Cotton Residence in Vienna. A large number of Vienna's prestigious 19th century blocks in the Ringstrasse zone are currently being extended into luxurious residences. Mostly, the result is alien UFOs landing on the historical roofs, with no reference to the existing structures and substance. Schenker Salvi Weber developed one of the best and most respectful solutions for such a project. They chose and found the language of "continued building", to which one can ascribe an architectural and aesthetic sustainability that will gradually transform into the reassuringly beautiful perception of a natural, urban entity.

This already expresses a stance that analyses with great precision the typological and morphological parameters of the location of every building task. It is also true for the two most important constructed projects by Schenker Salvi Weber to date, namely the Sillblock housing development in Innsbruck and the "Rochus" post office building in Vienna.

In the case of the Sillblock, it is their reaction to the urban planning situation that called for a closed block perimeter development. However, Schenker Salvi Weber divide the building into two wings, opening up the view from the street to the four protected linden trees in the communal courtyard to create a central urban element. The key aspect is the deliberately contrary formulation of the street and courtyard façade: outwardly closed and inwardly open.

But this decision was not merely based on emotional and empathetic motivation: it was also strategic. The striking inward-facing façade, which is waved with loggias, allows each apartment to aggressively participate in the public space. That may sound banal, but represents enormous spatial potential by moderate means. The extensive, closed balustrades also interpret the exterior space of the

lichen Hof zu einem zentralen urbanen Element. Entscheidend ist die bewusst konträre Formulierung der Strassen- und der Hoffassade: aussen geschlossen, innen frei.

Doch nicht nur emotional und emphatisch erfolgte diese Entscheidung, sondern strategisch. Die markant durch die Loggien gewellte Fassade zum Innenraum der Bebauung erlaubt jeder Wohnung eine offensive Teilnahme am öffentlichen Raum. Das klingt banal, ist aber ein räumliches Angebot, das mit geringem Aufwand ein enormes Potenzial bietet. Die flächig geschlossenen Brüstungen deuten zudem den Aussenraum der Wohnung als Teil des inneren Raums, der wiederum sehr genau überlegte mehrfache Sichtbeziehungen zum Aussenraum ermöglicht.

Dann das Projekt der Post am Rochus. Es ist einer der besten Bauten der letzten Jahre in Wien. Warum? Weil man ihm das auf den ersten Blick nicht ansieht. Der Auftrag war ein Glücksfall für Schenker Salvi Weber. Ein engagierter und mutiger Bauherr, die Österreichische Post AG, lobte einen geladenen Wettbewerb aus, den Schenker Salvi Weber gewannen. Um die heutigen Vergaberichtlinien zu erfüllen, musste sich das damals ökonomisch schwachbrüstige Büro Schenker Salvi Weber in der Entwicklung mit den Architekten von feld72 zusammenschliessen und das Statikbüro Gmeiner Haferl konnte solidarisch die dafür nötige Umsatzgarantie beisteuern. Seis drum.

Der Bauherr hatte sich entschieden, mit seiner Firmenzentrale nicht in ein anonymes Office-Quartier ins Niemandsland zu ziehen, sondern mitten in der Stadt eine eigene Liegenschaft mit einem Bauteil aus den 1920er-Jahren, dessen Fassade unter Denkmalschutz stand, zu nutzen. Auch der Standortvorteil war evident: U-Bahn-Haltestelle und ein etablierter Markt vor dem Bau, einfach mitten in der Stadt.

Unaufgeregt fügten sich Schenker Salvi Weber in die bestehende städtebauliche Struktur ein, nutzten aber den grossen Block für eine reichhaltige Binnenlandschaft mit grosszügigen Erschliessungsräumen, Höfen und Atrien. Dass der Bauherr die Erdgeschosszone mit Geschäften und Lokalen sozusagen der Stadt zurückgegeben hat, ist ein urbaner Gewinn. Dass der Bauherr aber auch den Architekten die Gestaltungsmöglichkeit und Möblierung der Bürogeschosse erlaubte, ist ein glücklicher Sonderfall für ein pragmatisches und effizientes Gesamtkunstwerk mit eleganter Gestaltung. Gelungen ist die atmosphärische Gliederung im heute angesagten Open Space mit Ruheinseln. Aber die Struktur ist robust genug, um in Zukunft auch andere Gliederungen und Nutzungen zu erlauben.

apartments as part of the interior space, thereby creating several very carefully considered visual relationships with the exterior space.

Then there is the Post am Rochus office project. It is one of the best Viennese buildings in recent years. Why? Because it is not apparent at first glance. The contract was a piece of good fortune for Schenker Salvi Weber. A committed and courageous client, the Austrian postal services, announced an invitation competition, which Schenker Salvi Weber won. To fulfil today's procurement regulations, the then economically lightweight office of Schenker Salvi Weber had to join forces with the architects of feld72 during the development stage and obtain support from the structural physics office Gmeiner Haferl to guarantee the necessary turnover. Be that as it may.

Instead of moving its headquarters to an anonymous office district in the middle of nowhere, the client decided to use its own real estate in the city centre, a 1920s building with preservation-listed façades. The advantages of the location were obvious, with an underground station and an established market in front of the building, simply in the midst of town.

Schenker Salvi Weber calmly integrated the project into the existing urban development structure, while using the largest block for a diverse interior landscape with spacious entrance foyers, courtyards and atria. The urban landscape gains from the fact that the client has as it were returned the ground floor zone to the city by filling it with shops and gastronomy. Furthermore, the client's willingness to leave the design and furnishing of the office floors to the architects is another positive exception that creates a pragmatic, efficient Gesamtkunstwerk with an elegant design. Today's popular open space with its peaceful islands has a successful atmospheric structure. But that structure is robust enough to allow other arrangements and uses in the future.

Yet the innovative aspects are the load-bearing structures of the building and the façade. Yes, at first glance, the building looks like the grid façades that are widespread throughout Europe and represent what will undoubtedly be regarded as a stylistic element of the period in terms of art-historical classification. However, it is actually a glass façade with load-bearing columns behind it and a superimposed concrete grid. It includes in its vertical elements the shafts for naturally ventilating the interior rooms, which are flush when closed and also create small circular apertures. Furthermore, the dimensions of the elements change on different floors. This is a conscious architec-

Doch die Innovationen sind die statische Struktur des Gebäudes und die Fassade. Ja, der Bau schaut auf den ersten Blick so aus wie die heute in ganz Europa gängigen Rasterfassaden, die unwidersprochen als Stilelement der Epoche kunsthistorische Einordnung bekommen werden. Aber es ist eigentlich eine Glasfassade mit tragenden Säulen dahinter und einem vorgeblendeten Betonraster. Dieser inkludiert in seinen vertikalen Elementen Lüftungsflügel zur natürlichen Belüftung der Innenräume, die einerseits geschlossen glatt und andererseits mit kleinen kreisförmigen Öffnungen versehen sind. Zudem verändern sich die Masse der Elemente im Verlauf der Geschosse. Es handelt sich deshalb um eine bewusste architektonische Gliederung, um ein Raster mit Mehrwert und Geheimnis sozusagen.

Diese virtuos subtilen architektonischen Manöver erinnern mich an die abklingende Moderne, als die plakativ radikalen Konzepte der Anfangszeit an der Wirklichkeit des Bauens scheiterten und zu einem angemessenen architektonischen Umgang mit dem Neuen im Vorhandenen führten. Der Schweizer Architekt Otto Salvisberg war so ein Meister der Angemessenheit. Als «Architektur auf den zweiten Blick» wurden seine Methode und Haltung bezeichnet. Vielleicht können oder sollen wir heute wieder aus dieser Position neue kreative Kraft schöpfen, nicht arrogant und plakativ ankämpfen gegen das Vorhandene, uns eitel in Szene setzen, sondern Parameter des Vorhandenen akzeptieren und dem eine neue Sicht und Schicht anlehnen, die eine Kontinuität des Urbanen und der Architektur nachvollziehbar erlaubt.

Ich komme zurück zu meiner eingangs erwähnten Skepsis gegenüber heutigen Positionen zeitgenössischer Architektur. Es gibt keine glaubwürdigen Manifeste und Deklarationen mehr. Es gibt keine ausufernden intellektuell philosophierenden, metaphorisch poetischen Erklärungen mehr. Schenker Salvi Weber zeigen uns dagegen, dass man sich pragmatisch der Instrumente und Verfahren der Moderne heute bedienen und damit eine Architektur entwickeln kann, die konzeptionell innovativ (ich hasse diesen Begriff) doch neue architektonische Verhältnisse schafft und diese mit dem vielleicht derzeit noch unbewusst Vorhandenen thematisieren und verbinden kann. «Out of the box» eben. Sie wissen nicht warum, ich weiss nicht warum, aber es liegt ein Geheimnis in ihrer Architektur, das mich fasziniert und sich eben nicht auf den ersten Blick, sondern in der Zeit erschliesst. Das ist es doch, was wir uns wünschen: eine schöne und intelligente Architektur, an der wir uns bis in alle Ewigkeit erfreuen können.

tural structuring measure to give the grid added value and a certain element of mystery.

The accomplished, subtle architectural manoeuvre reminds me of declining Modernism, when the striking, radical concepts of its beginnings were defeated by the reality of building and led to an appropriate architectural handling of new aspects in existing structures. The Swiss architect Otto Salvisberg was one such master of appropriateness. His method and approach was described as "architecture at a second glance". Perhaps today, we can or should draw new creative power from that position, instead of arrogantly using eye-catching methods to fight against what already exists; rather than vainly staging ourselves, the aim is to accept the parameters of what is there and give it a new perspective and layer, thereby making both the continuity of the urban structures and the architecture perceptible.

I return to my initially expressed scepticism towards today's positions of contemporary architecture. There are no longer any plausible manifestos or declarations. There is no longer any expansive intellectual philosophising, no more metaphoric, poetic descriptions. However, Schenker Salvi Weber show us that today, one can use the instruments and processes of Modernism pragmatically and thereby develop architecture that is conceptually innovative (though I hate the term) and yet create new architectural conditions, addressing them and connecting them to what already exists, but has not yet been consciously perceived. In other words, thinking "out of the box". They do not know why and nor do I, but there is a secret in their architecture that fascinates me, one which is not apparent at first glance, but is only revealed over time. After all, that is what we are seeking: beautiful, intelligent architecture that pleases us for ever.

Wohnbebauung Sillblock, Innsbruck, Tirol

Sillblock housing development, Innsbruck, Tyrol

Vier Linden.
Im ehemaligen Schlachthofgebiet soll die Blockrandbebauung aus den 1920er-Jahren wieder aufgenommen werden. Strassenseitig fügt sich die U-Form unauffällig in den städtischen Raum, nach innen umfasst der zweigeteilte, sich verjüngende Baukörper einen neuen, attraktiven Hof rund um die bestehenden Lindenbäume.

Harte Schale/weicher Kern.
Der Schwerpunkt des Entwurfs liegt in der klaren Trennung von Strasse und Hofraum. Die weiche Schale holt die Bewohner an der Strasse ab und begleitet sie in den Hofraum. Die schlanken Enden und dicken Ecken generieren eine konkave Form als Visavis zur mächtigen Nordkette.

Balkonarena.
Die letzte Schicht zum Hof bildet die Balkonarena – eine geschwungene Fassade aus Betonfertigteilen, eine robuste Aneignungsschale zum Sich-Einwohnen.

Wohnteppich.
Das ganze Gebäude baut sich in Schichten um die Wohnungen bis in den Stadtraum auf und wird insgesamt zu einem Volumen mit Tiefe und vielfältigen räumlichen Qualitäten.
Die Qualität der Wohnungen liegt in der teppichartigen Grundrissstruktur und Flexibilität.

Italomodern.
Materialität, Form und Farben werden dort eingesetzt, wo sie identitätsstiftend wirken oder funktionale Ansprüche verdeutlichen. Eine Sehnsucht nach der nahen Ferne – nach dem Italomodernen der Gebrüder Feiersinger – soll entstehen.

Four linden trees.
On the grounds of the former abattoir, the block perimeter development from the 1920s is to be reoccupied. On the street side, the U-shaped building is unobtrusively integrated into the urban space. The two-winged, narrowing building frames an attractive new courtyard around the existing linden trees.

Hard shell/Soft core.
The focus of the design lies in the clear distinction between the street and the courtyard space. The soft shell receives the residents at the street and accompanies them to the courtyard space. The slim end and thick corners create a concave form to face the powerful northern mountain range.

Balcony arena.
The final layer towards the courtyard is formed by the balcony arena, a robust appropriating shell for making oneself at home.

Living carpet.
The entire building develops in layers around the apartments to become an overall volume with depth and diverse spatial qualities.
The apartments' quality lies in the carpet-like floorplan structure and flexibility.

Italian modernism.
Materials, form and colours are applied where they strengthen identity or highlight functional requirements. The aim is to achieve a yearning for distant lands – for the Italian modernism of the Eiersinger brothers.

Wettbewerb / Competition: 2010
Ausführung / Construction: 2012–2014
Auftraggeber / Client: Innsbrucker Immobilien Gesellschaft, Innsbruck AT

Statik / Statics:
Baumann + Obholzer Ziviltechniker, Innsbruck AT
Bauleitung & Kosten / Construction management & Costs: IIG – Immobiliengesellschaft der Stadt Innsbruck, Innsbruck AT
Bauphysik & Akustik / Structural physics & Acoustics: Spektrum – Zentrum für Umwelttechnik, Innsbruck AT
Elektroplanung / Electro-planning: Elektrotechnische Planung, Wien AT
Gebäudetechnik / Building technology: Technisches Büro Hermann Hofer, Innsbruck AT
Landschaftsplanung / Landscape architecture: Barbara Bacher, Linz AT

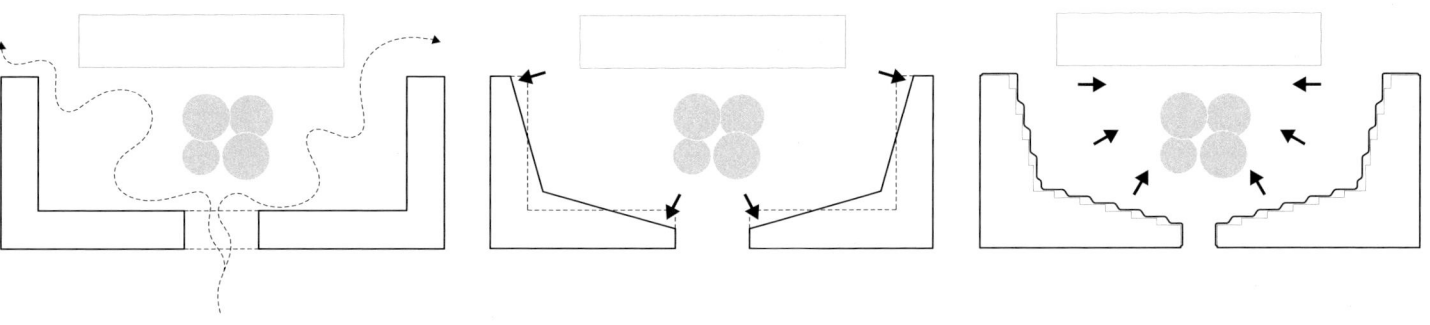

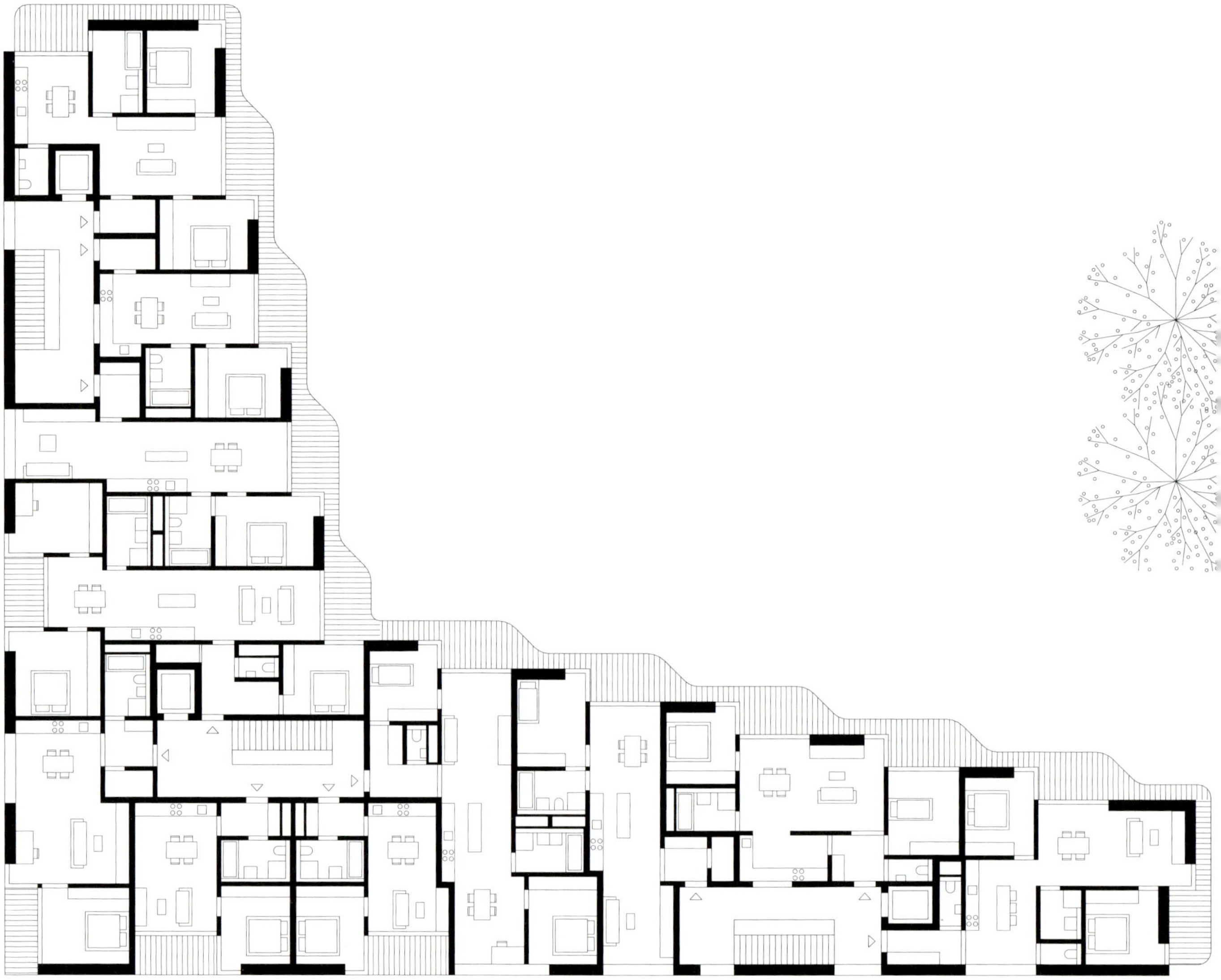

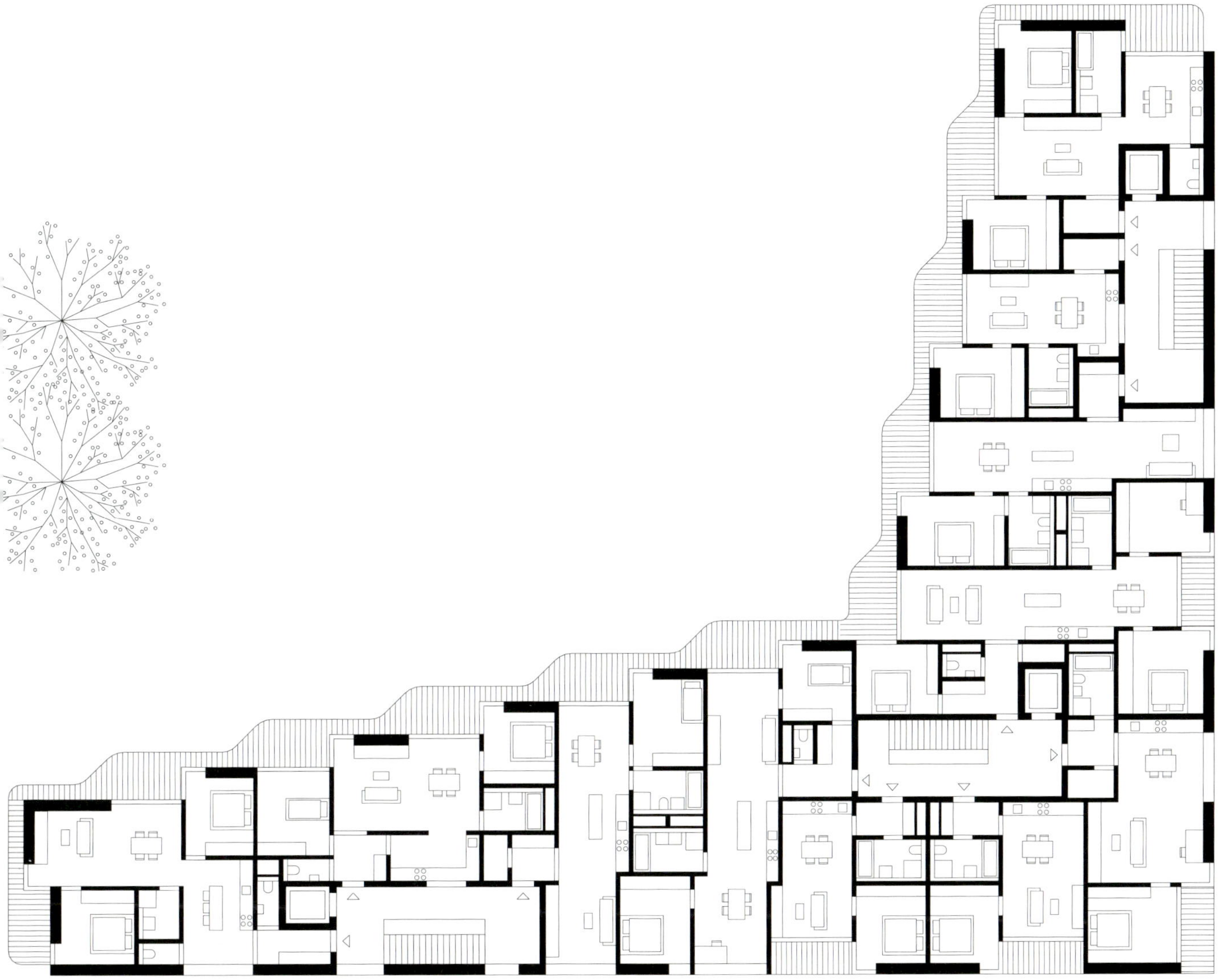

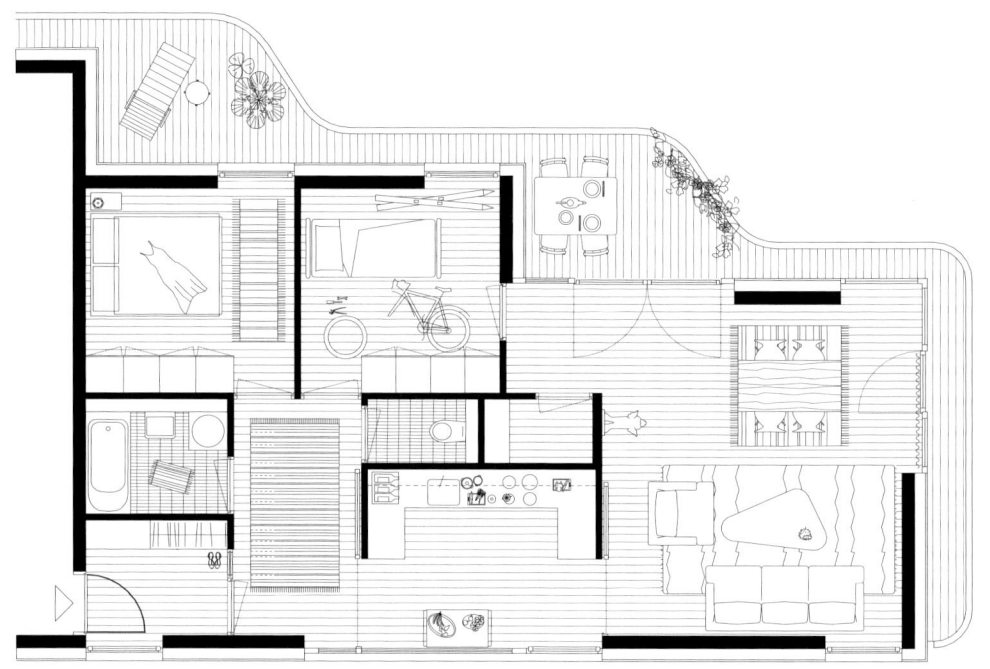
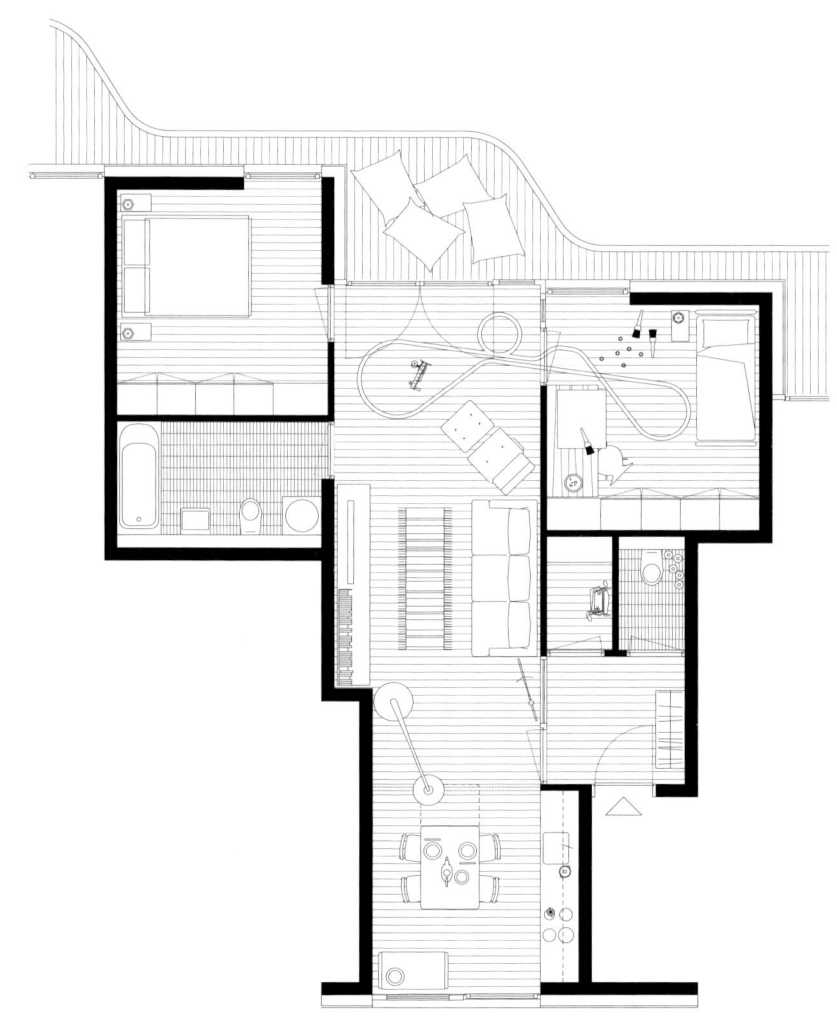

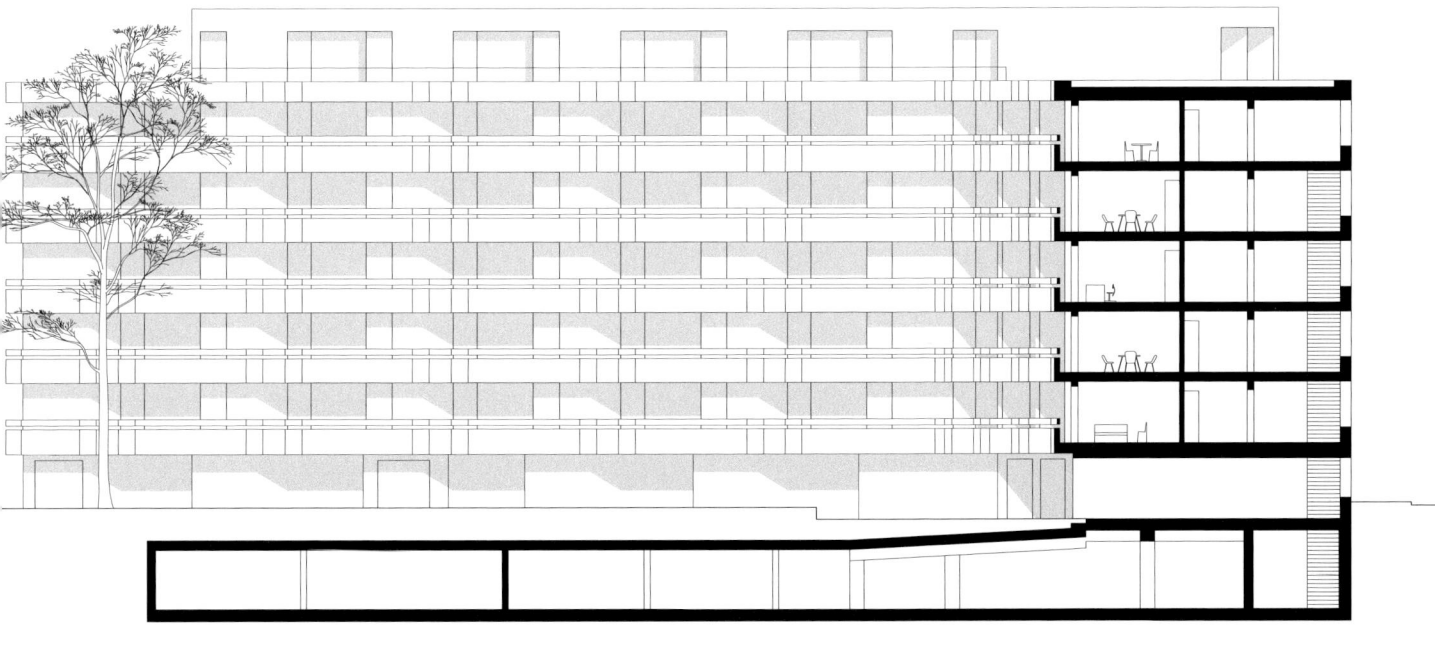

Post am Rochus, Wien

Post am Rochus, Vienna

Der Stadtbaustein.
Die Post als wichtige Institution des öffentlichen Lebens präsentiert sich als Stadtbaustein mit einer dezent plastisch ausformulierten Fassade und stimmig proportionalem Baukörper mit zwei Innenhöfen und Terrassen.

Architektur als Hintergrund.
Durch die haptische Materialität wie durch das ruhige nuancierte Spiel der Fassade erzeugt das neue Gebäudeensemble für das Leben am Rochusmarkt eine unaufgeregte und dennoch starke Präsenz im Hintergrund.

Das Kleid.
Die unregelmässigen Perforierungen in den Fensterlaibungen dienen unter anderem zur Belüftung und geben der vorfabrizierten Fassade aus sandgestrahlten Betonfertigteilen ihren Charakter. Je nach Tageszeit und Sonnenstand zeigt die Fassade ein anderes Gesicht.

Die Atriumsfuge.
Der Neubau wird durch eine mehrgeschossige, atriumartige Fuge an den denkmalgeschützten Altbau aus den 1920er-Jahren angedockt. Sie dient als zentrale Erschliessung für das gesamte Ensemble. Es entsteht eine Raumdramaturgie mit offenen Kommunikationszonen und klar definierten Rückzugsbereichen.

Der öffentliche Weg.
Die Platzebene des Rochusmarktes setzt sich als Mall im Gebäude fort und bindet als öffentlicher Durchgang an den Grete-Jost-Park an. Durch die zwei grossen, dominanten, ovalen Oberlichte über den Rolltreppen wird die Mall über die Innenhöfe belichtet.

Die Bürolandschaft.
Eine flexible Bürolandschaft für tausend PostmitarbeiterInnen. Büroutensilien wandern am Feierabend in die Spinde. Eichenholz, leichte Vorhänge, hochflorige Teppiche, warme Farben, eigens von uns entworfene Möbelsegmente: akustisch wirksam, gediegen und elegant.

An urban building block.
The post office, an important institution of public life, presents itself as an urban building block with a subtly sculptured façade formulation and a coherently proportional building volume with two interior courtyards and terraces.

Architecture as a background.
With its haptic materials and the calm, nuanced interplay of the façades, the new building ensemble creates a composed, yet powerful presence in the background.

The gown.
The irregular perforations in the window apertures also aid ventilation and give the façade made of sand-blasted prefabricated concrete elements its character. The façade presents a different expression depending on the time of day and the angle of the sun.

The atrium joint.
The new structure is docked onto the existing 1920s building by means of a multi-storey, atrium-like joint. It serves as the central entrance for the entire ensemble, consisting of a dramatic spatial composition with open communication zones and clearly defined areas for withdrawal.

The public path.
The square level of the Rochusmarkt continues within the building as a mall and provides a public connecting walkway to the Grete Jost Park. The two large, dominant, oval skylights above the escalators provide natural light from the interior courtyards.

The office landscape.
A flexible office landscape for a thousand post office employees. Office tools wander in the lockers at the end of the working day. Oak wood, light curtains, highly floral carpets, warm colours and furniture segments designed specially for us: acoustically effective, tasteful and elegant.

Wettbewerb / Competition: 2013
Ausführung / Construction: 2013–2017
Auftraggeber / Client: Österreichische Post, Wien AT

Kooperation / Cooperation:
Architektur / Architecture: feld72 Architekten, Wien AT
Statik / Statics: Gmeiner Haferl Bauingenieur, Wien AT
Bauphysik & Akustik / Structural physics & Acoustics: IBO – Österreichisches Institut für Bauen und Ökologie, Wien AT
Gebäudetechnik / Building technology: team gmi, Wien AT
Brandschutz / Fire protection: IMS Brandschutz, Wien AT
Lichtplanung / Lighting design: Christian Ploderer, Wien AT
Landschaftsplanung / Landscape architecture: DnD Landschaftsplanung, Wien AT

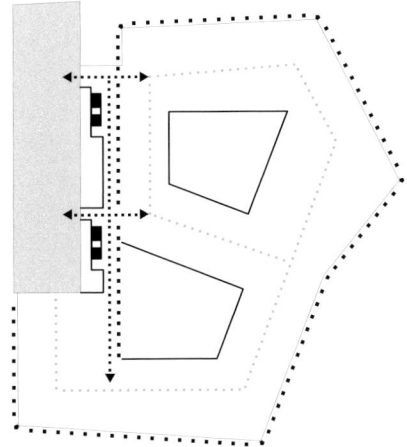

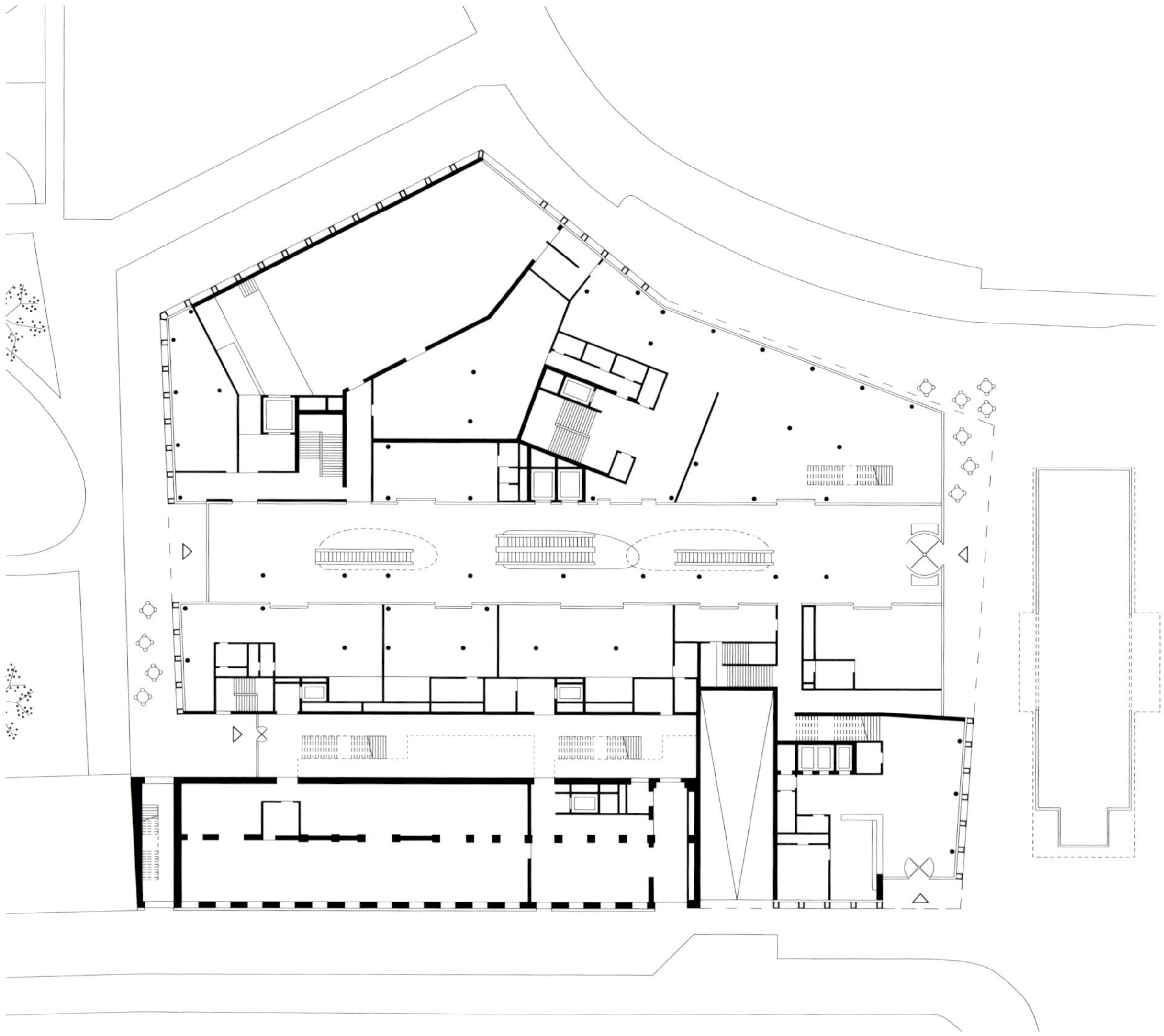

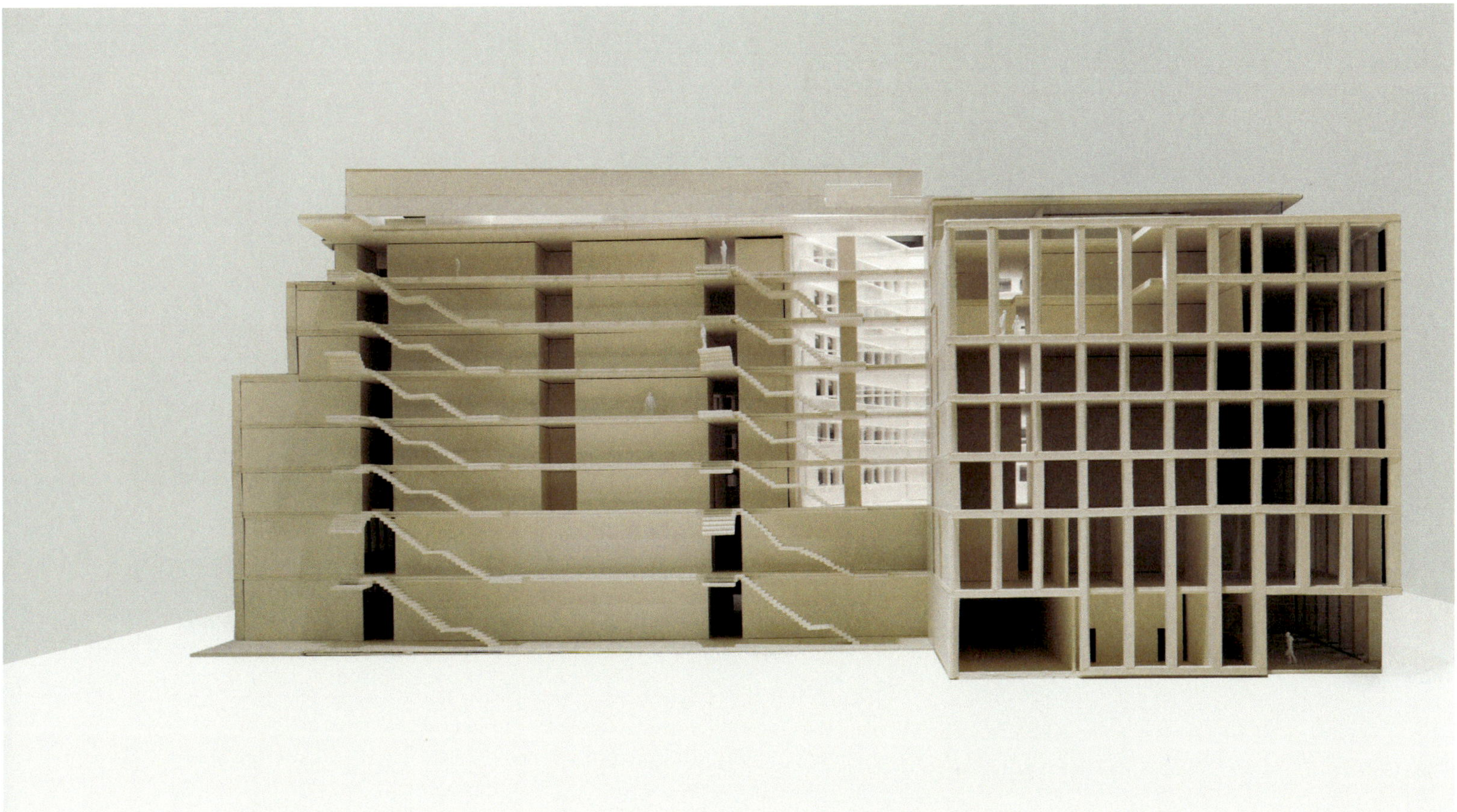

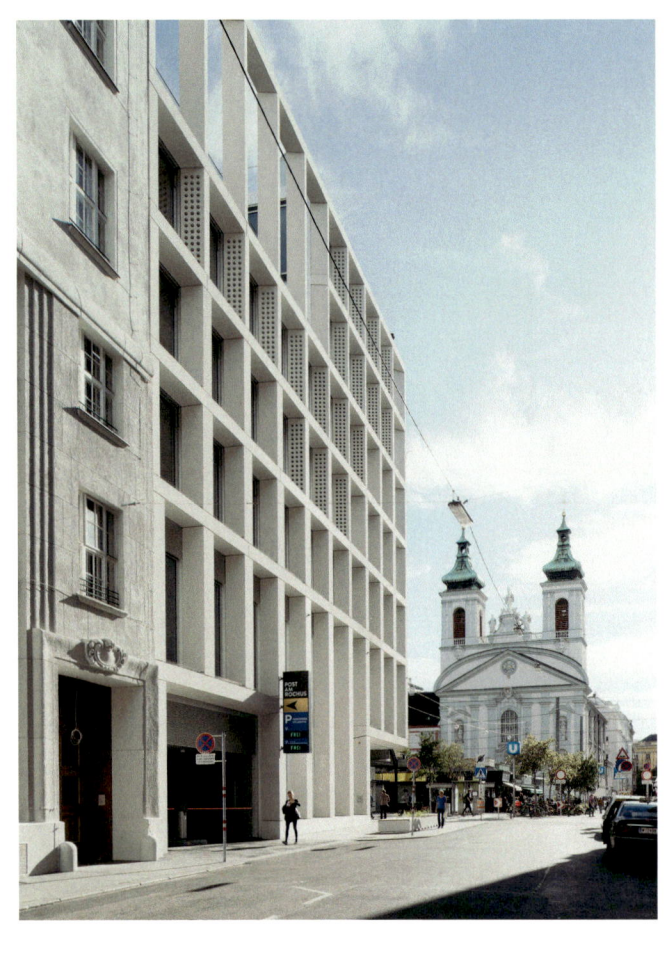

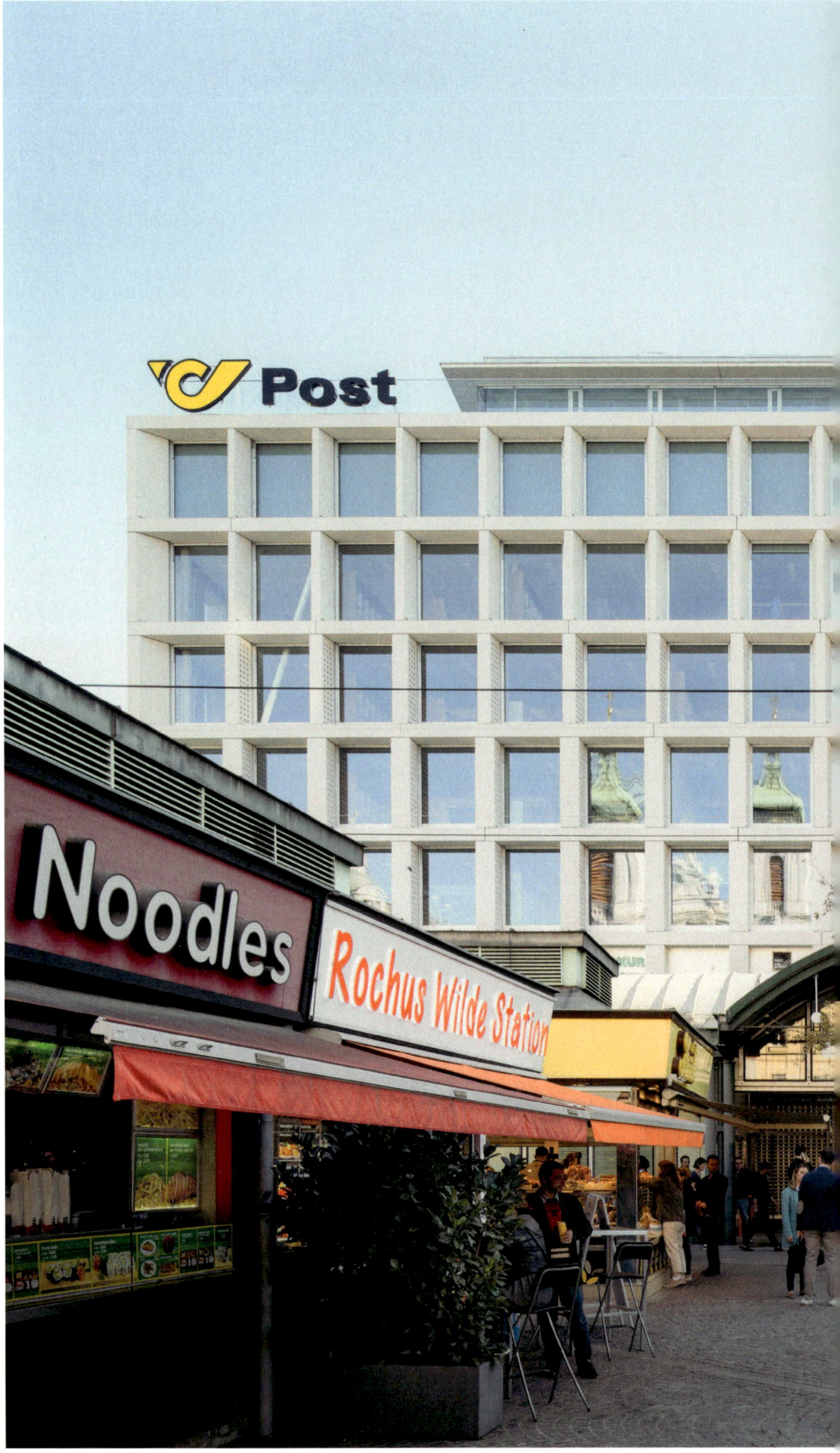
Post
Noodles
Rochus Wilde Station

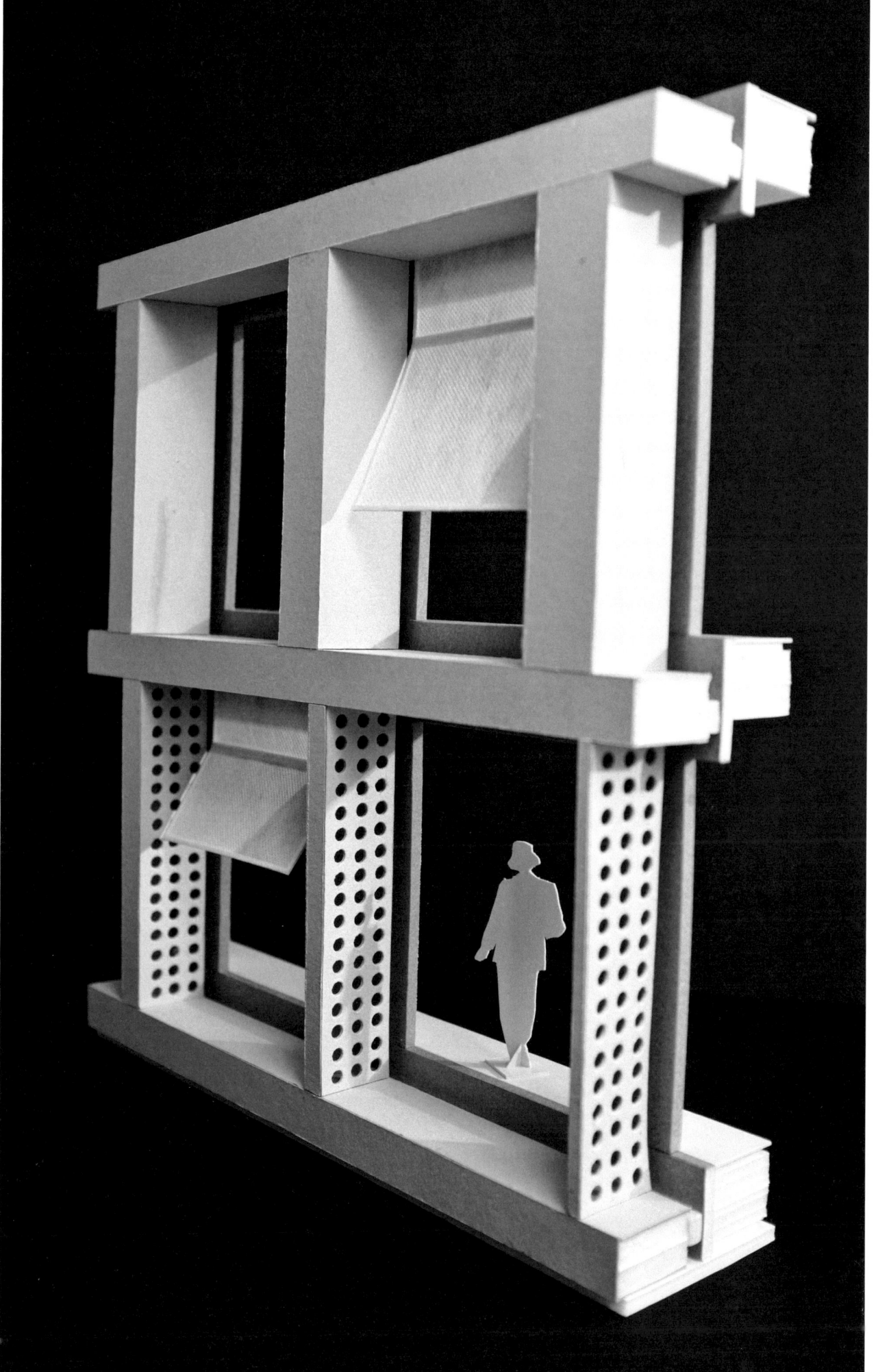

Volksschule Absam Dorf, Absam, Tirol

Absam Village Primary School, Absam, Tyrol

Platz schaffen.
Viel Programm, wenig Platz – das war die Ausgangslage für die Dreifachturnhalle mit Kindergarten und Musikschule in Absam am Fusse des Karwendelgebirges. Die denkmalgeschützte Schule eingespannt zwischen Kirche, Friedhof und Berg.

Leicht über schwer.
Gegen alle Zweifel: Das riesige Turnhallenvolumen wurde ins Erdreich vertieft und schafft dort eine eigene mineralische, zenital belichtete Welt. Der leichte Holzbau schiebt sich über den leeren, schweren Bauch im Grund und spannt gemeinsam mit dem Bestand einen neuen Platz fürs Dorf auf. Dieser ist abwechselnd Pausenhof, Sommerkino, Flohmarkt.

Wolf im Schafspelz.
Der neue Baukörper ordnet sich ein und spinnt die Materialität des Ortes weiter. Ein verputzter Holzbau schwindelt sich ins Ensemble. Die alte Reibputztechnik in Kalkzement verleiht ihm ein taktiles Äusseres. Feiner und rauer Putz ergänzen sich und verorten die Löcher im Pelz.

Die dritte Haut.
Gebündelte Raumeinheiten generieren eine kontinuierliche, alternierende Raumfigur. In der Mitte sitzen drei trichterförmige Oberlichtkanonen. Die so belichtete dritte Haut in Eiche, Filz und lackiertem Holz begleitet durch den Raum. Die hüpfenden Fenster laden zum Sitzen und Schauen ein. Der Ort ist latent vorhanden.

Trompetenkolonnade.
Die Musikschule soll in den denkmalgeschützten leeren Dachstuhl. Die Fenster müssen klein sein. Die Idee entwickelt sich aus der Problematik. Die trompetenförmigen Raumeinheiten kreuzen sich – bilden eine Raumstruktur und führen in den zeltförmigen Veranstaltungsraum. Das Konzert kann beginnen.

Creating space.
A full programme, little space – that was the initial situation for the triple sports hall with a kindergarten and music school in Absam at the foot of the Karwendel mountain range. The preservation-listed school is inserted between the church, the cemetery and the mountain.

Light over heavy.
Overcoming all doubt: the enormous sports hall volume was sunken into the earth, thereby creating its own mineral world that is naturally lit by overhead light. The lightweight timber structure slides over the empty, heavy belly in the ground, forming a new square for the village in combination with the existing structure. It is used alternately as a playground, a summer cinema and a flea market.

Wolf in sheep's clothing.
The new building integrates itself into the existing structures and picks up on the materials of the location. A plastered timber building deceives its way into the ensemble. The old float-finish plastering technique using lime cement gives it a tactile exterior. Fine and coarse plaster complement each other and locate the perforations in the coat.

The third skin.
Pooled spatial units generate a continuous, alternating spatial figure. Three funnel-shaped skylight cannons are situated in the centre. The third skin in oak, felt and varnished wood guides visitors through the space. The hopping windows invite you to sit and gaze. The location is latently present.

Trumpet colonnade.
The music school is planned for the preservation-listed, empty roof structure. The windows must be small. The idea is developed out of the problem. The trumpet-shaped spatial units cross – forming a spatial structure and leading to a tent-like event room. Let the concert begin.

Wettbewerb / Competition: 2013
Ausführung / Construction: 2014–2016
Auftraggeber / Client: Gemeinde Absam

Kooperation / Cooperation:
Statik / Statics: Merz Kley Partner, Dornbirn AT
Bauphysik & Akustik / Structural physics & Acoustics: IBO – Österreichisches Institut für Bauen und Ökologie, Wien AT
Bauleitung & Kosten / Construction management & Costs: Die Bauleiter, Innsbruck AT
Gebäudetechnik / Building technology: Moser + Partner Ingenieurbüro, Absam AT
Landschaftsplanung / Landscape architecture: DnD Landschaftsplanung, Wien AT

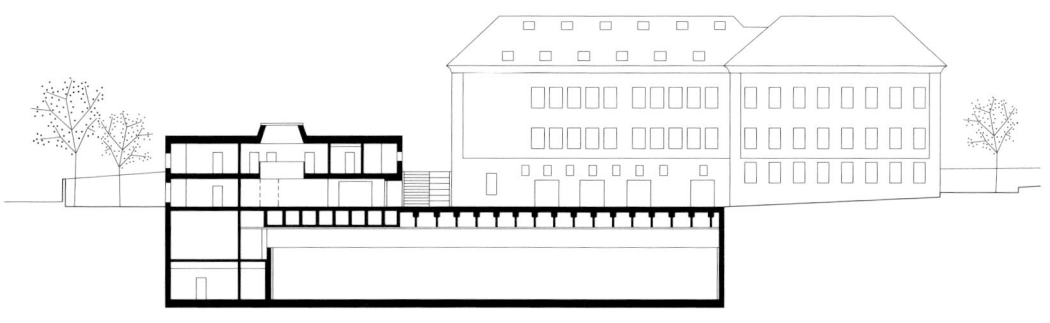

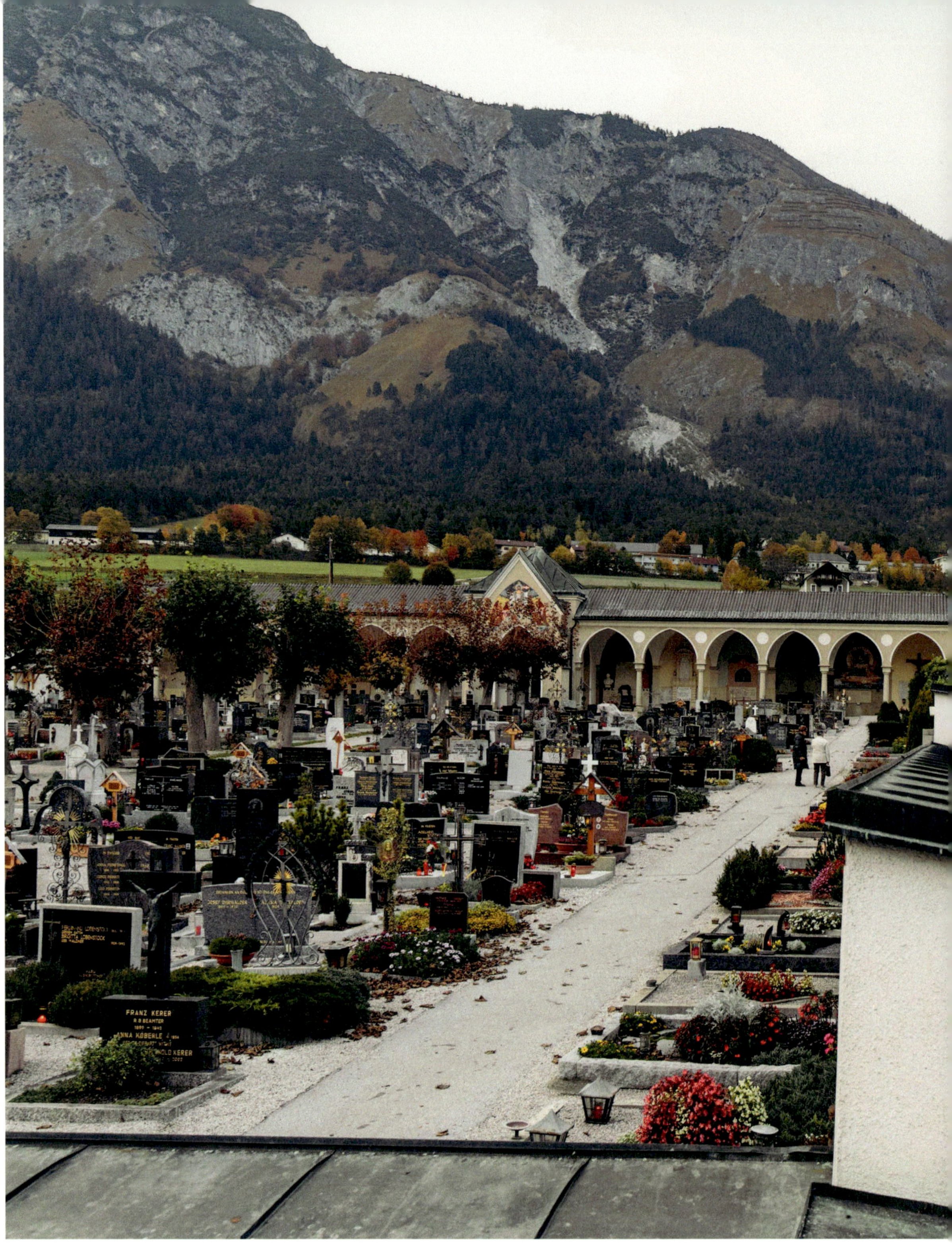
FRANZ KERER

ERWIN WIRTENBERGER

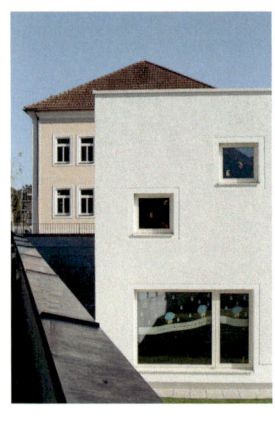

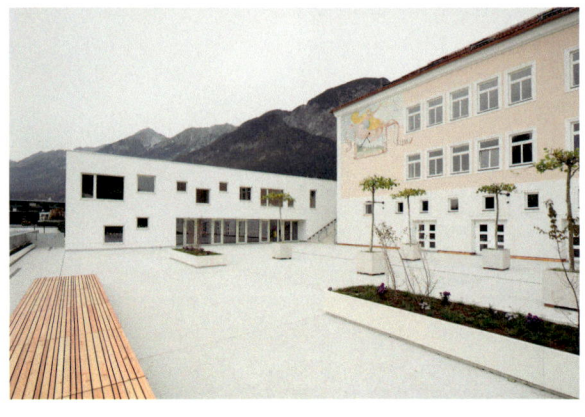

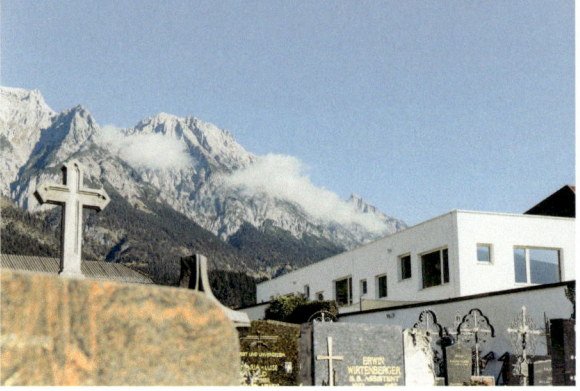

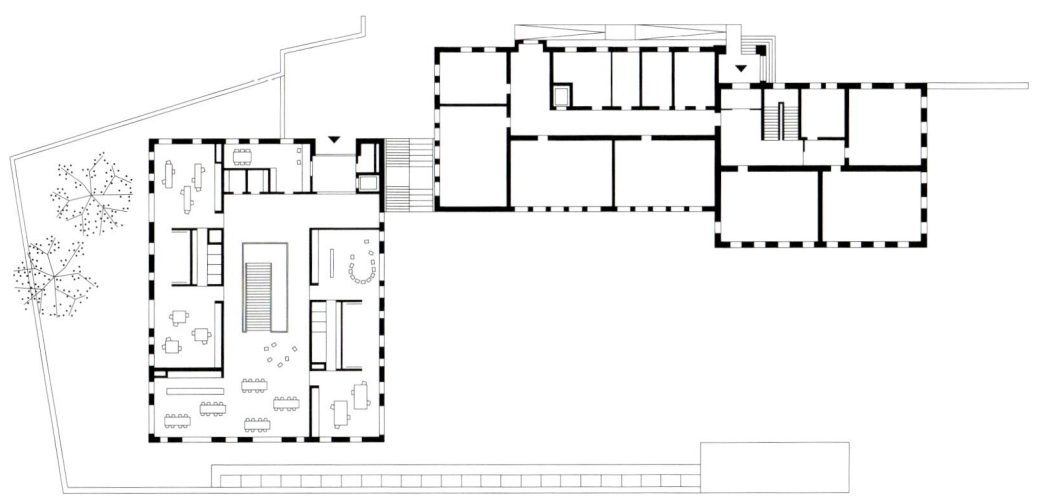

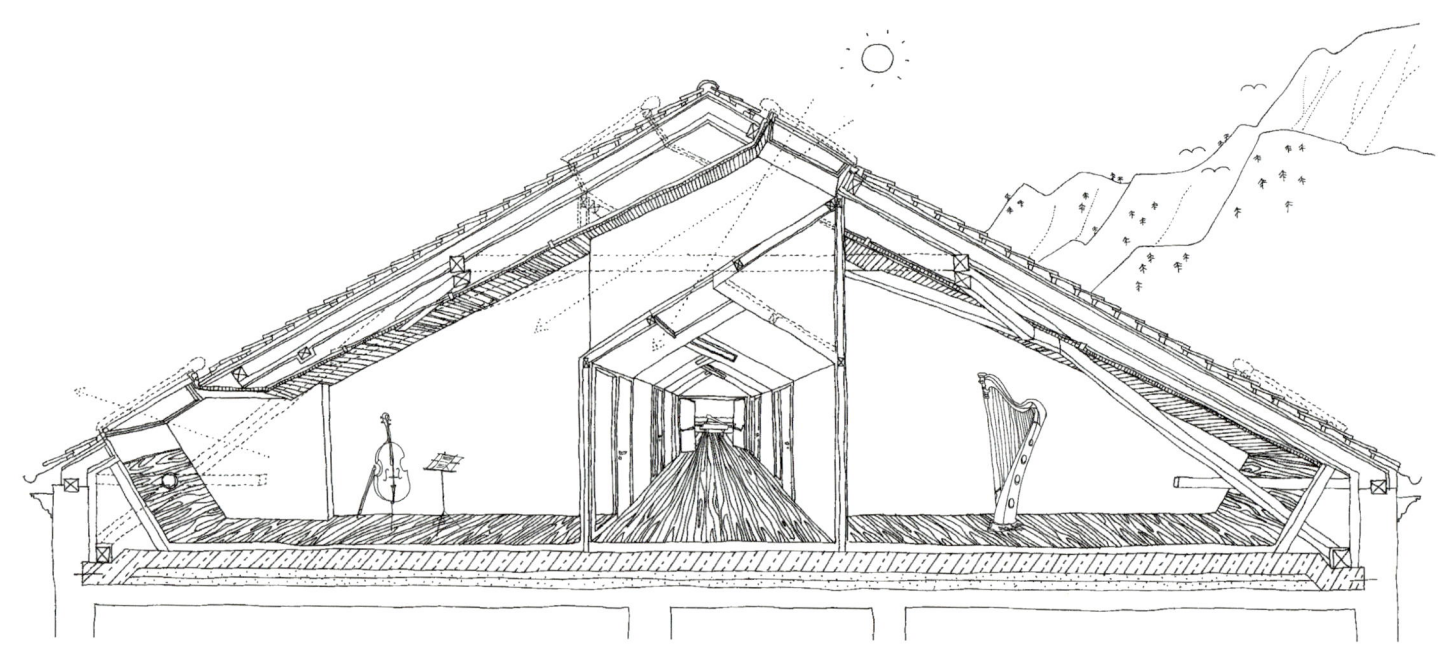

Haus S, Ehingen, Baden-Württemberg

Verzahnen.
Das Wohnhaus positioniert sich bewusst zentral auf dem Grundstück. Alle Räume erhalten einen lebendigen Bezug zum Garten und zum räumlichen Umfeld. Die Verknüpfung erfolgt durch allseitig eingeschnittene Terrassen. Innen- und Aussenraum verzahnen sich.

Präzise Kerben.
Die in den Betonkörper eingeschnittenen Raumsequenzen sind verglast und maximal transparent. Es etabliert sich ein stimmungsvolles, lichtdurchflutetes Ambiente. Die Kerben verbinden Innen und Aussen. Der aufgespannte Hof ergänzt das Raumangebot und bildet die introvertierte Mitte.

Flacher Grundriss.
Der Grundriss dehnt sich in der Fläche aus und bildet eine klare Raumstruktur. Es entsteht eine flexible Wohnlandschaft. Alles ist auf einer Ebene, Aussen und Innen, gewohnt wird dort, wo es gerade passt.

Gestufter Schnitt.
Im Wohnbereich, mit über vier Metern Raumhöhe, wird die Verflechtung der unterschiedlichen Höhen zum räumlichen Erlebnis. Der tiefe Bauteil verankert sich im hohen Bauteil. Eine Schwelle lädt zum Betreten der so entstandenen Wohnbühne ein.

Raumhaltiger Stein.
Dem stringenten Grundriss steht ein klares Materialkonzept zur Seite. Homogen in Sichtbeton ausgeführt, steht das Haus als raumhaltiger Stein im Garten. Im Inneren webt sich die tertiäre Schicht in die entstandenen Ecken und Kanten. Rohbau und Ausbau reichen sich die Hand.

House S, Ehingen, Baden-Württemberg

Interlocking.
The residential building has a deliberately central position on the property. All rooms have a lively reference to the garden and the spatial environment. The connection is achieved by incised balconies on all sides. Interior and exterior spaces interweave.

Precise incision.
The spatial sequences incised into the concrete volume are glazed and have a maximum transparency, establishing an atmospheric mood that is suffused with light. The apertures connect the inside and outside. The spanned courtyard enhances the spatial variety and creates an introverted centre.

Flat ground plan.
The ground plan spreads out over the areas and forms a clear spatial structure to create a flexible residential landscape. Everything is on one level, outside and inside. Life takes place where it is right at that moment.

Staggered section.
In the living area, with a room height of over four metres, the intertwining different heights become a spatial experience. The deep building element is anchored in the tall structure. A threshold invites visitors to enter the living stage it creates.

Voluminous stone.
The stringent ground plan is supported by a clear material concept. Constructed homogeneously in fair-faced concrete, the house stands like a voluminous stone in the garden. Inside, the tertiary layer weaves itself into the created corners and edges. The shell construction and its finish go hand in hand.

Wettbewerb / Competition: 2010
Ausführung / Construction: 2011–2013
Auftraggeber / Client: Privat / private

Kooperation / Cooperation:
Bauleitung & Kosten / Construction management & Costs: Architekturbüro zwo P, Ulm DE
Statik / Statics: JR Consult, Graz AT
Bauphysik & Akustik / Structural physics & Acoustics: IBO – Österreichisches Institut für Bauen und Ökologie, Wien AT

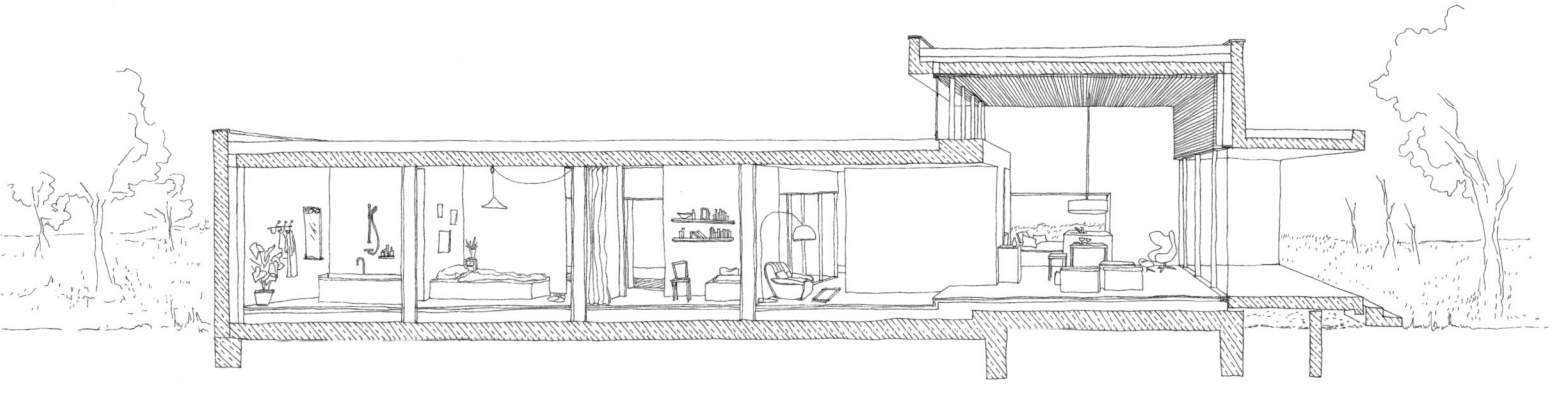

48

Heime der Franziskanerinnen, Wien

"Heime der Franziskanerinnen" old people's home, Vienna

Vier Quader und Rand.
Vier quadratische Volumen werden durch ein Rückgrat zu einer Grossform verbunden.
Die Setzung am Rand der Bebauungslinie schafft eine wohltuende Trennung zwischen Öffentlichkeit und intimerem Therapiepark. Der dreigeschossige Baukörper wird terrassiert in den Hang eingebettet.

Park und Hang.
Die gebaute Landschaft wird Teil des Hügels. Die Ebenen knüpfen an den Park im Hang an und laden zu Spaziergängen ein. Die alten Bäume prägen die Stimmung am Ort. In einer entspannten Atmosphäre geniesst man den Blick über Wien.

Wohnen und Gruppe.
Um einen zentralen Wohnbereich ordnen sich radial die Individualzimmer an. Nutzungen überlagern sich, eine familiäre Atmosphäre entsteht. Der bewachsene Patio baut einen latenten Bezug zum Haus auf. Die daran angelehnte Küche bildet das Herz der Gruppe.

Mikro und Makro.
Die Zimmer sind Rückzug mit Kontakt zum Aussenraum. Die Fenster im Leibungsmöbel sind tief und hoch.
Das kleinste Vielfache als Mikroeinheit in einer dichten Wohn- und Lebenssituation. Es geht darum, die Nähe und die Distanz in einem räumlichen Makrosystem zu moderieren.

Schiff und Berg.
Die geschossweise gestaffelte Holzbaufassade webt die Fenster der Individualzimmer subtil in den Baukörper ein. Die Holzfarbe osziliert zwischen Bronze und Silbergrau. Ein Spiel aus horizontalen und vertikalen Stäben hilft dem Schiff über den Berg.

Four cuboids and an edge.
Four quadratic volumes are connected by a backbone to create a larger form.
The ensemble's placement at the edge of the development line creates a pleasant distinction between public space and the more intimate therapy park. The three-storey building is terraced and embedded into the slope.

Park and slope.
The developed landscape becomes part of the hill. The level areas pick up on the park on the slope and invite people to walk there. The old trees characterise the atmosphere of the location, allowing one to enjoy the view of Vienna in a relaxed environment.

Living and group.
The individual rooms are arranged radially around a central living area. Uses overlap, creating a familiar atmosphere. The overgrown patio generates a latent reference to the house. The kitchen is inspired by it, forming the heart of the group.

Micro and macro.
The rooms are a retreat, while maintaining contact with the exterior space. The windows are deep and high, creating furniture in the apertures.
The smallest multiplication as a micro-unit in a dense residential and living situation. The aim is mediating between the nearness and distance in a spatial macro-system.

Ship and mountain.
The staggered floors of the timber façade subtly weave the windows of the individual rooms into the building volume. The colour of the wood oscillates between bronze and slivery grey, creating an interplay of horizontal and vertical rods to help the ship over the mountain.

Wettbewerb / Competition: 2016
Ausführung / Construction: 2017–2019
Auftraggeber / Client: Franziskanerinnen von der christlichen Liebe, Wien AT

Kooperation / Cooperation:
Statik / Statics: Tragwerkplanung Freller, Klagenfurt AT
Projektmanagement / Project management: Bauwert Köstenberger, Metnitz AT
Bauphysik & Akustik / Structural physics & Acoustics: IBO – Österreichisches Institut für Bauen und Ökologie, Wien AT
Gebäudetechnik / Building technology: Technisches Büro Herbst, Gleisdorf AT
Elektroplanung / Electrical engineer: Ingenieurbüro Tauß, Grafendorf bei Hartberg AT
Brandschutz / Fire protection: IMS Brandschutz, Wien AT
Landschaftsplanung / Landscape architecture: DnD Landschaftsplanung, Wien AT

Volksschule Bütze, Wolfurt, Vorarlberg
Bütze Primary School, Wolfurt, Vorarlberg

Ort im Ort.
Wolfurt ist ein klassisches Vorarlberger Strassendorf. Die zu erweiternde Schule steht abseits dieser Strasse in der Mitte des Dorfteils Bütze, einem Ort im Ort.

Romantische Erinnerung.
Der jüngere eingeschossige Bauteil besticht durch seine romantisch anmutenden Höfe und seine ausladenden Vordächer mit Stützenkolonnade. Schwer und schnell gealtert, muss er dennoch weichen.

Eine Lernlandschaft.
Die Idee basiert auf der romantischen Erinnerung. Eine ursprüngliche Gangschule wird zu einem fliessenden, mäandrierenden Teppich. Der wird mit hofartigen Patios und Oberlichten durchwirkt. Die Lernlandschaft bietet latent Orte an.

Alt und Neu.
Was ist alt? Was ist neu? Man weiß es nicht. Die Lernlandschaft generiert eine Stimmung, nicht einen Hinweis. Trotzdem gibt es – auf den zweiten Blick – eine taktile Fährte, wie Alt und Neu erscheint.

Programm schafft Raum.
Der Neubau in Holz spannt sich mit dem raumhaltigen Obergeschoss über die alte Turnhalle. Der Eingang wird in den neuen Schwerpunkt der Anlage verschoben. Hier warten Garderoben, Eltern-Café und Mittagstisch. Die Nutzungen stehen durch die vorgeschlagene Raumstruktur in permanenter Beziehung zueinander.

Ein Haus.
Die geschossweise subtil gestaffelte Holzfassade fasst das Volumen zusammen. Die Schichtung hilft dem Haus um die Ecke. Ausnahmen bestätigen die Regel – Fensterformate betten sich ein. Die Pergola zieht die Fassade auseinander. Es entsteht ein Zwischenlernraum. Er knüpft an die Geschichte des Ortes an.

Village within a village.
Wolfurt is a classic Vorarlberg linear settlement. The school extension is situated away from the street in the centre of the part of the village known as Bütze, a village within a village.

Romantic reminiscence.
The more recent, enclosed building section is striking in terms of the romantic appearance of its courtyards and its projecting canopies with a colonnade. The heavy and quickly ageing structure had to make way for the extension.

A learning landscape.
The idea is based on romantic reminiscence. An original school with a central corridor becomes a fluent, meandering carpet. It is permeated with courtyard-like patios and skylights. The learning landscape offers latent locations.

Old and new.
What is old? What is new? It is unclear. The learning landscape instils an atmosphere without any clues. Nevertheless, closer inspection reveals a tactile trace of the old and new.

Programme creating space.
The new timber building spans its voluminous upper storey over the old sports hall. The entrance is moved to the new focus of the facility, providing changing rooms, a parents' café and lunch. The uses are in a state of permanent communication due to the proposed spatial structure.

A house.
A subtly stacked timber façade frames the volume. The layering helps the house around the corner. Exceptions prove the rule – window formats embed themselves. The pergola pulls the façade apart. There is an intermediary space for learning that picks up on the history of the location.

Wettbewerb / Competition: 2015
Ausführung / Construction: 2017–2018
Auftraggeber / Client: Gemeinde Wolfurt

Kooperation / Cooperation:
Statik / Statics: Hämmerle – Huster, Bregenz AT
Bauphysik / Structural physics: IBO – Österreichisches Institut für Bauen und Ökologie, Wien AT
Gebäudetechnik / Building technology: GMI Peter Messner, Dornbirn AT
Elektroplanung / Electrical engineer: Ingenieurbüro Hiebeler + Mathis, Hörbranz AT
Brandschutz / Fire protection: IMS Brandschutz, Wien AT
Landschaftsplanung / Landscape architecture: DnD Landschaftsplanung, Wien AT

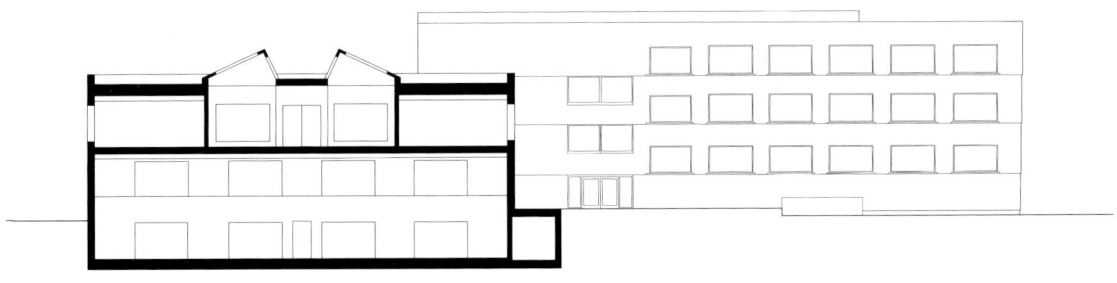

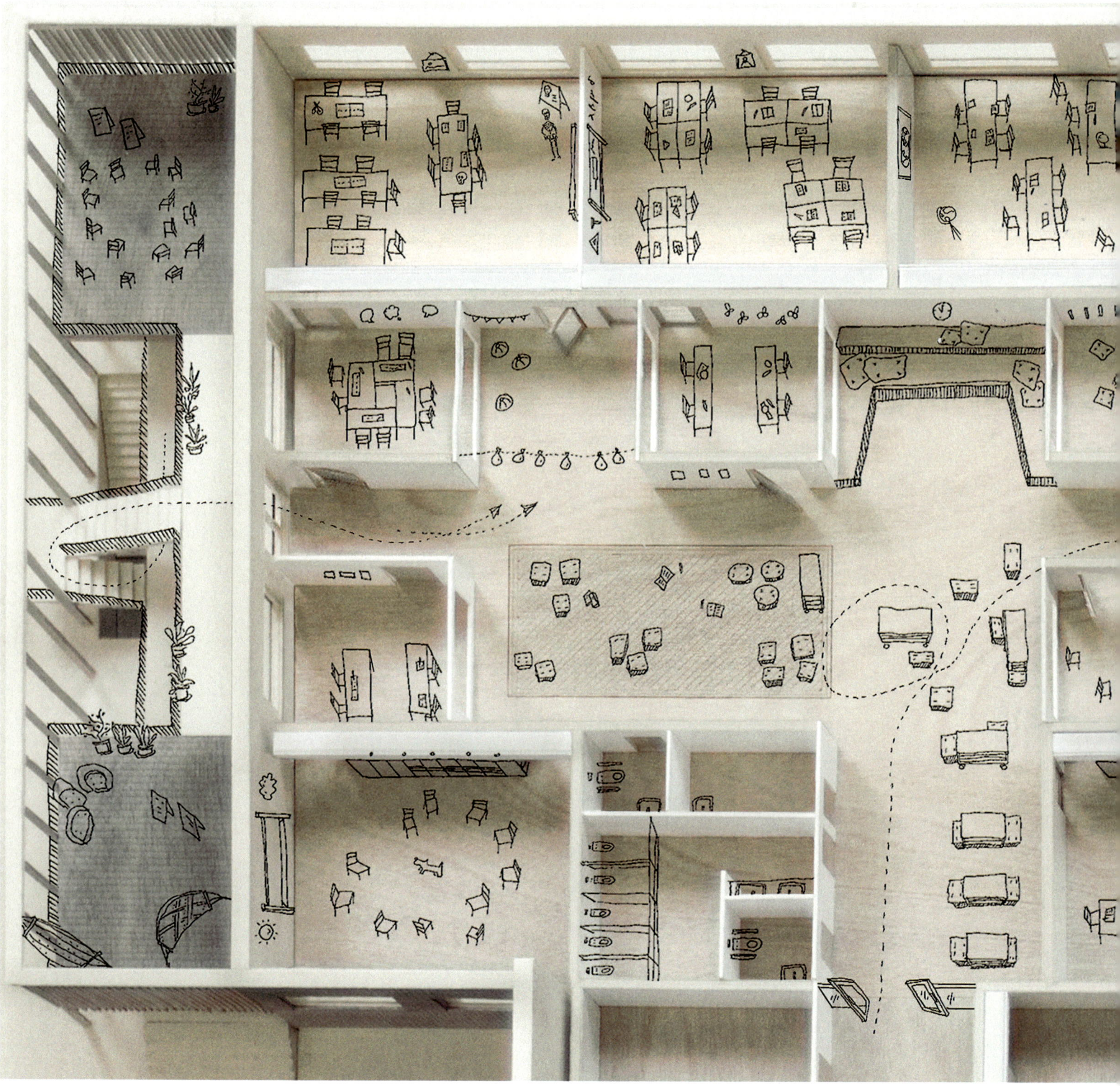

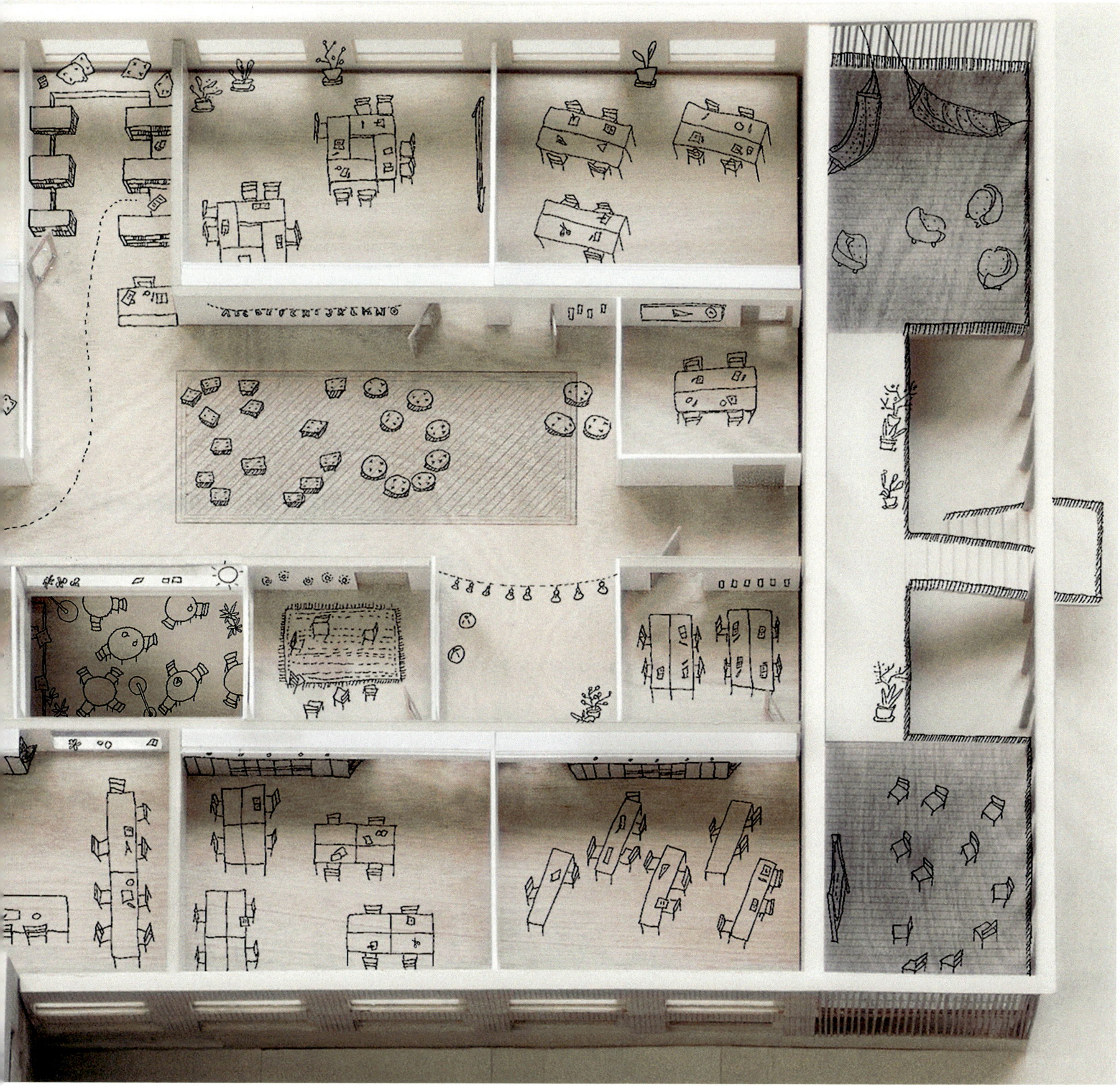

Zinshaus Neutorgasse, Wien
Rented apartment building, Vienna

Das Palais.
Das denkmalgeschützte Gebäude im ehemaligen Wiener «Fetzenviertel» beherbergte neben Wohnungen einst die Verkaufslokale der Baumwoll- und Zwirnspinnerei Harlander. Bis 2018 wird das – bis vor kurzem von der Telekom genutzte – Haus im 1. Bezirk umgebaut und wieder zu dem, was es einst war: ein Wohnhaus mit hochwertigen Apartments – nur ohne Textilfabrik.

Glamouröse Nebenrolle.
Hauptakteure bleiben die historischen Eckrisalite und Türme. Der unaufgeregte Dachausbau fügt sich mit Understatement in seine glamouröse Nebenrolle. Als räumliches Implantat setzt er sich zwischen die historische Struktur.

Das Zaubergeschoss.
Durch die Absenkung der Decke über dem vierten Obergeschoss entsteht ein zusätzliches fünftes Vollgeschoss mit Panoramablick und grosszügigen Terrassen. Diese raumhaltige Fuge klappt an ihren Rändern nach oben und wird unerwartet zum Aussenraum. Es entsteht eine grosszügige, natürlich belichtete Wohnebene zwischen Alt und Neu.

Wien-Panorama.
Von aussen sind die Terrassen und grossen Panoramafenster dezent in den Baukörper integriert. Im Innenraum spannen sich Cinemascope-Ausblicke über Wien. Die Dachlandschaft setzt sich als Nest zwischen Donaukanal und Stephansdom.

Typologische Vielfalt.
Die in die robuste Bestandsstruktur eingewobenen Wohnungen bieten reizvolle Typologien wie Turmzimmer, Erker und Balkone. Es entsteht eine elegante Interpretation eines gründerzeitlichen Wohnpalais im historischen Herzen Wiens.

The palais.
The preservation-listed building in the Viennese former textile quarter known as the "Fetzenviertel" used to house apartments and also the stores selling products by the Harlander cotton and yarn spinning mill. By 2018, the house in the 1st District – which was recently used by Telekom – will be converted and restored to what it once was: a condominium with high-quality apartments – just without the textile factory.

Glamorous supporting role.
The main protagonists remain the historical corner projections and the towers. The reserved roof conversion assumes its glamorous supporting role with understatement. The spatial implant slots in between the historical structures.

The magical floor.
Lowering the ceiling over the fourth floor enables a full additional fifth floor with a panorama view and large terraces. This spatial joint folds upwards at the edges to surprise the exterior space. The result is a spacious, naturally lit residential floor that moves between old and new.

Vienna panorama.
From the outside, the terraces and large panorama windows are subtly integrated into the building. Cinemascope views of Vienna can be enjoyed in the interior. The rooftop landscape sits like a nest between the Danube canal and St. Stephen's Cathedral.

Typological diversity.
The apartments are interwoven into the robust existing structure, offering attractive typologies such as tower rooms, bay windows and balconies. The result is an elegant interpretation of a 19th century apartment palais in the historical heart of Vienna.

Wettbewerb / Competition: 2014
Ausführung / Construction: 2016–2018
Auftraggeber / Client: Österreichische Post, Wien AT

Kooperation / Cooperation:
Architektur / Architecture: feld72 Architekten, Wien AT
Statik & Bauphysik / Statics & Structural physics: FCP – Fritsch Chiari & Partner, Wien AT
Gebäudetechnik / Building technology: BPS Engineering, Wien AT
Brandschutz / Fire protection: FCP – Fritsch Chiari & Partner, Wien, Berlin

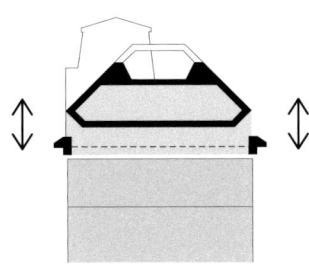
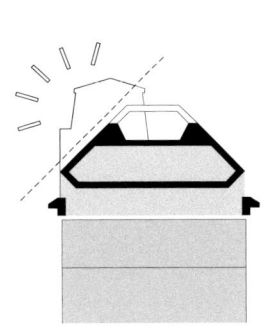
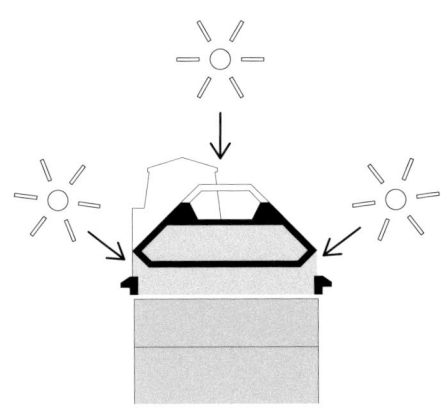

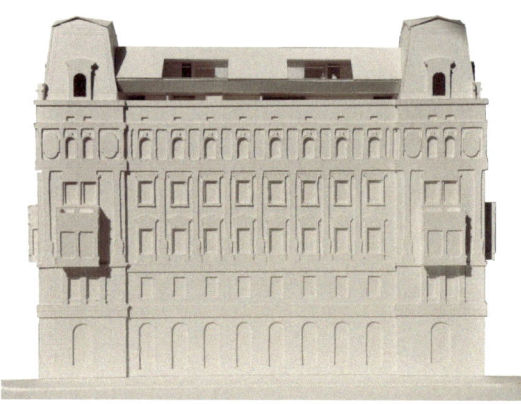
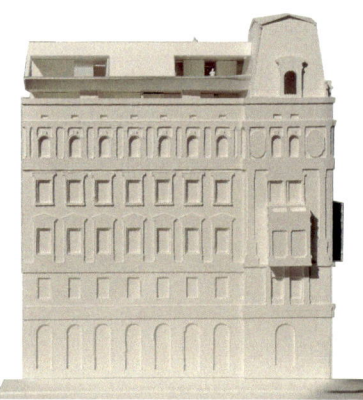

Teehaus, Wien

Tea house, Vienna

Klause.
Ein Rückzugsort mit intimer Stimmung für gemütliche Gespräche im Trubel der Vienna Contemporary. Ein ruhiger Ort im hektischen Kunstmessen-Alltag.

Eins-zu-eins-Modell.
Das Teehaus will nicht Skulptur sein. Es will mehr Modell als gebaute Realität sein.
Innen und Aussen divergieren. Der Massstab wird verschoben und ist trotzdem stabil. Graukartonschindeln decken das Holzhaus ein, eine stimmungsvolle Leuchte setzt einen mittigen Akzent und bündelt die Runde.

Tea und Talk.
Das Teehaus auf schwarzen Stelzen. Beinpaare der Sitzenden mischen sich unter die Stützenfüsse. Der kreisförmige Ausschnitt als Sitzbank. Auf rundem Filz die Teekanne. Das warme Holz in Kontrast zur grellen Umgebung. Das Gespräch kann beginnen.

Naive Form.
Das Objekt als schnell erfahrbare archaische Figur. Kreisformen überschneiden sich mit einem Würfel. Die Konstellation führt zu einer einfachen, starken Urtypologie. Nach dem gebückten Eintreten durch das klein gehaltene Loch eröffnet sich den Besuchern im Inneren eine ganz andere Welt. Geborgenheit unter einem kaminartigen Oberlicht. Es entsteht ein Gleichgewicht der Teile.

A retreat.
A place of withdrawal with an intimate atmosphere for relaxed conversations in the hubbub of Vienna contemporary. A peaceful place in the hectic everyday art-fair life.

One-to-one model.
The tea house is not intended as a sculpture. Instead it aims to be more a model than built reality.
The interior and exterior diverge. The scale is shifted and is nevertheless stable. Grey board shingles cover the timber building, while an atmospheric light adds central accentuation and has a pooling effect.

Tea and talk.
The tea house on black stilts. The seated guests' pairs of legs mingle with the building's support feet. The circular section is used as a bench. The teapot rests on round felt. The warm wood contrasts with the bright environment. Let the conversation begin.

Naive form.
The building as a quickly graspable archaic figure. Circular forms overlap with a cube. The constellation leads to a simple, powerful original typology. After bending over to enter through the deliberately small hole, visitors discover a completely different world inside. Security beneath a chimney-like skylight. A balance between the elements is achieved.

Ausführung / Construction: 2017
Auftraggeber / Client: C/O Vienna Magazine / Redaktionsbuero Ost, Wien AT

Kooperation / Cooperation:
Tischlerei / Carpenter: Wolfgang Prohaska, Wien AT
Modellbau / Model construction: Modellwerkstatt Gerhard Stocker, Wien AT

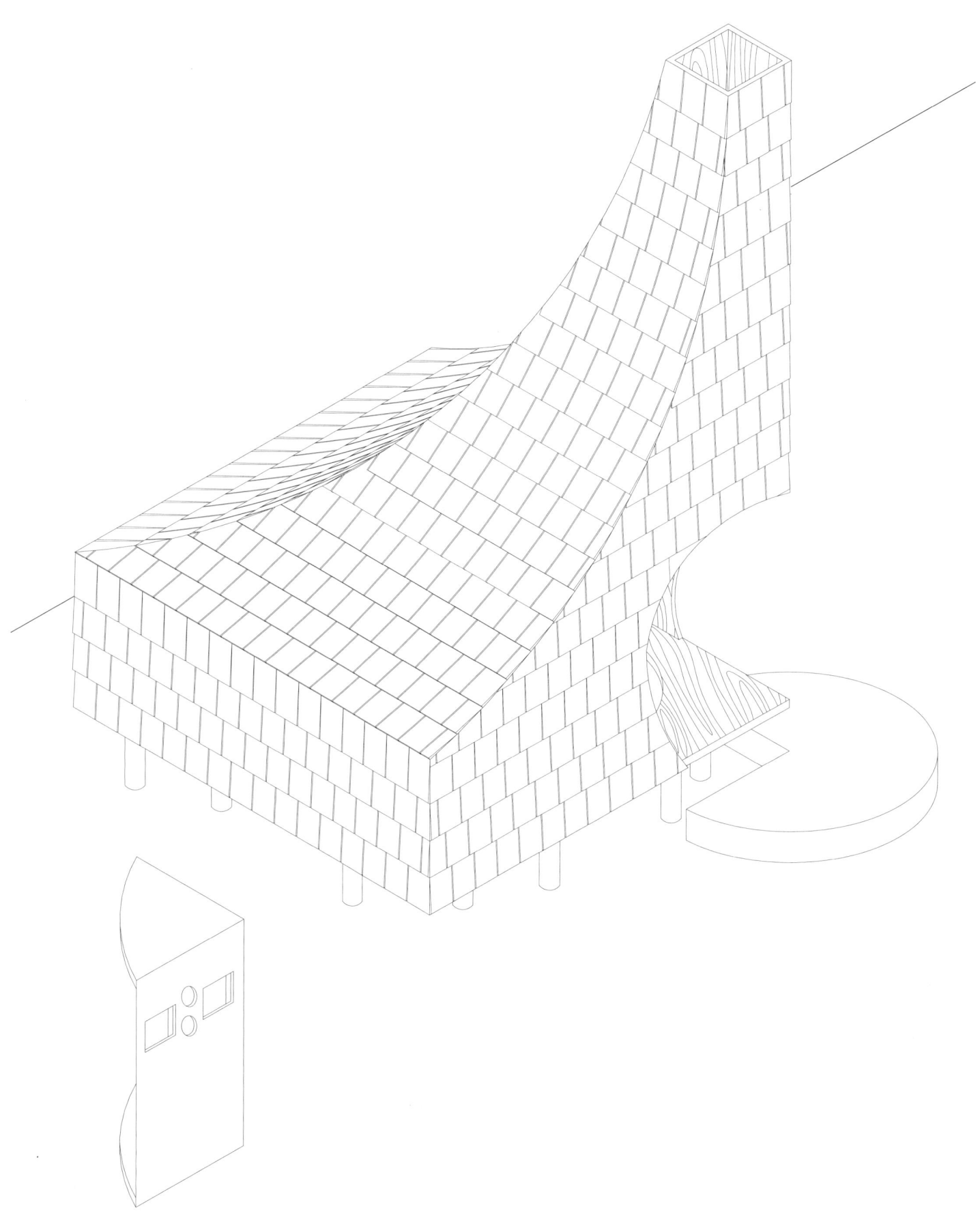

Werkverzeichnis / List of works
Auswahl Bauten, Projekte und Wettbewerbe / Selection of buildings, projects and competitions

2010	1	Wettbewerb Pavillon Oberried, Belp CH (1. Preis); in Zusammenarbeit mit SSSVT Architekten, Bern CH Wettbewerb Restaurant Mangolds, Graz AT (1. Preis)
	2	Wettbewerb Wohnüberbauung Brünnen, Bern CH (4. Preis) Wettbewerb Basisschule Schalmenacker, Rafz CH (4. Preis) Installation Melktribüne, Melk AT
2011	3	Wettbewerb Wohnen im Ostviertel, Aachen DE (3. Preis); in Zusammenarbeit mit Daniel Payer Architektur, Berlin DE Wettbewerb Wohnheim St. Joseph, Bremgarten CH (6. Preis)
2012	4	Wohnungsumbau Darwingasse, Wien AT
	5	Wettbewerb Schulanlage Ebnet, Embrach CH (2. Preis) Wettbewerb Wohnen München Riem, München DE (4. Preis) Büroumbau OSZE Vertretung, Wien AT

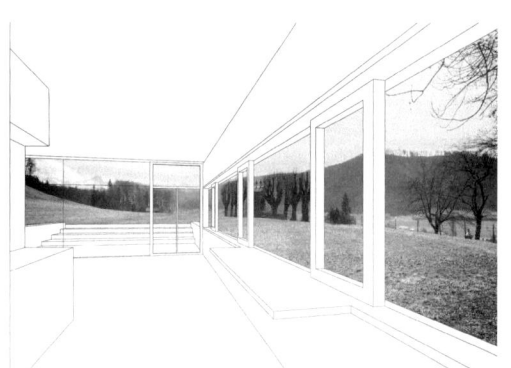

1

2

3

4

5

2013		Haus S, Ehingen DE (Wettbewerb 2010, 1. Preis)
	6	Wettbewerb Volksschule Kirchenfeld, Bern CH (3. Preis)
		Umbau Mehrfamilienhaus Elsässerstrasse, Basel CH;
		in Zusammenarbeit mit Architektur Dickmann, Basel CH
2014	7	Wettbewerb Rudolf Steiner Schule, Wien AT (3. Preis)
	8	Wettbewerb Alten- & Pflegeheim, Vöcklabruck AT
	9	Wettbewerb Schule und Sport Ried, Köniz CH
		Schulsanierung VS Reisnerstraße, Wien AT
		Wohnbebauung Sillblock, Innsbruck AT (Wettbewerb 2010, 1. Preis)
2015		Wettbewerb Landespflegeheim, Hainfeld AT (3. Preis)
		Wettbewerb Wohnbebauung Integrationshaus, Innsbruck AT;
		in Zusammenarbeit mit einszueins Architektur, Wien AT
		Wettbewerb Quartiershaus Sonnwendviertel, Wien AT
	10	Wettbewerb Medizinische Fakultät, Linz AT

6

7

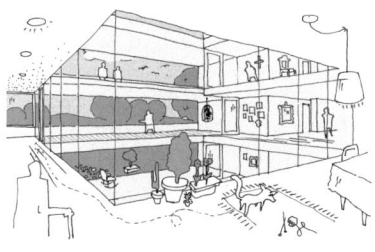
8

9

10

2016		Volksschule Absam Dorf, Absam AT (Wettbewerb 2013, 1. Preis)
		Wettbewerb Biologiezentrum Universität Wien, Wien AT
	11	Wettbewerb Volksschule Kundl, Kundl AT
		Installation Salon C/O Vienna Art Contemporary, Wien AT
2017		Post am Rochus, Wien AT (Wettbewerb 2013, 1. Preis); in Zusammenarbeit mit feld72 Architekten, Wien AT
		Wettbewerb Bildungscampus Carlbergergasse, Wien AT (Anerkennung)
	12	Wettbewerb Universität für Bodenkultur Boku, Wien AT (Anerkennung)
	13	Wettbewerb Bildungscampus Bürgerspitalwiese, Wien AT (Anerkennung)
	14	Wettbewerb Wohnbebauung Heidestraße, Berlin DE (3. Preis)
	15	Wettbewerb Landesleitzentrale Polizei, Linz AT (2. Preis)
		Wettbewerb Volksschule Wolkersdorf, Wolkersdorf AT (3. Preis)
		Installation Teehaus C/O Vienna Art Contemporary, Wien AT
2018		Wettbewerb Bürogebäude Zentrale Wien Kanal, Wien AT (Anerkennung)
		Wettbewerb Kunst- und Musikschule, Bad Vöslau AT (3. Preis)
		Wettbewerb Wohnhochhaus Nordbahnhof, Wien AT; in Zusammenarbeit mit Franz&Sue Architekten Wien AT

11

12

13

14

15

Laufende Projekte

16   Wohnheim Stiftung Aarhus, Gümligen CH (Wettbewerb 2012, 1. Preis)
     Zinshaus Neutorgasse, Wien AT (Wettbewerb 2014, 1. Preis);
     in Zusammenarbeit mit feld72 Architekten, Wien AT
     Volksschule Bütze, Wolfurt AT (Wettbewerb 2015, 1. Preis)
17   Umbau Bürohaus Praterstern 4 ÖBB, Wien AT (Wettbewerb 2016, 1. Preis);
     in Zusammenarbeit mit Günter Mohr Architekt, Wien AT
     Heime der Franziskanerinnen, Wien AT (Wettbewerb 2016, 1. Preis)
18   Schulzentrum FvS Rösrath, Rösrath DE (Wettbewerb 2016, 1. Preis);
     in Zusammenarbeit mit Felix Thörner Architekt, Düsseldorf DE
     Wohnbebauung Way 2 Smart, Korneuburg AT (Wettbewerb 2017, 1. Preis)
19   Wohnbebauung am Eisweiher, Lörrach DE (Wettbewerb 2017, 1. Preis)
     Wohnbebauung Waidmannsdorf, Klagenfurt AT (Wettbewerb 2018, 1. Preis);
     in Zusammenarbeit mit Clemens Kirsch Architektur, Wien
     Wohnhaus Wallrißstraße, Wien AT
     Büroumbau Wien Energie, Wien AT (Wettbewerb 2018, 1. Preis)

16

17

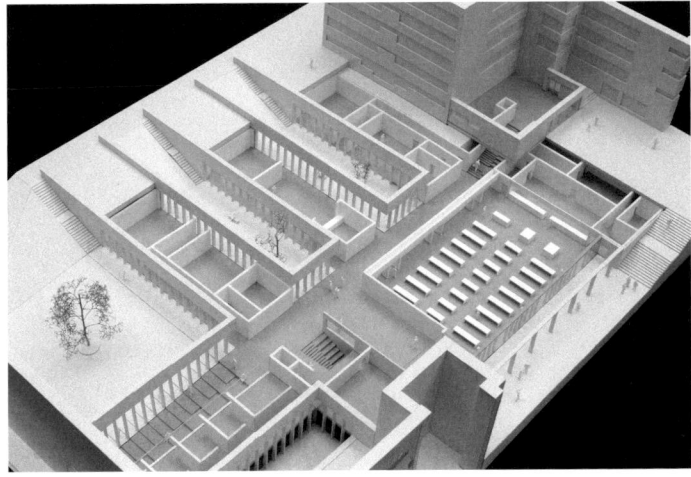
18

19

Andres Schenker

1978	geboren in Bern
1994–1997	Zeichnerlehre Bauart Architekten, Bern
1998–1999	Praxis bei SSSVT Architekten, Bern
2001	Accademia di architettura, Mendrisio
2002–2007	Universität für angewandte Kunst, Wien
2008	Zaha Hadid Architects, London
2009	Gründung von Schenker Salvi Weber ZT GmbH, Wien-Bern
2010	Mitglied des Schweizerischen Architektenvereins SIA
2013	Mitglied der Kammer der ArchitektInnen für Wien, Niederösterreich, Burgenland
1978	Born in Bern CH
1994–1997	Draughtsman's apprenticeship at Bauart Architects, Bern
1998–1999	Practical experience at SSSVT Architects, Bern
2001	Accademia di architettura, Mendrisio
2002–2007	University for Applied Arts, Vienna
2008	Zaha Hadid Architects, London
2009	Founded Schenker Salvi Weber ZT GmbH, Vienna - Bern
2010	Member of the Swiss Society of Engineers and Architects SIA
2013	Member of the Chamber for Civil Engineers and Architects for Vienna, Lower Austria and Burgenland

Michael Salvi

1974	geboren in Bern
1990–1993	Zeichnerlehre Schindler & Habegger Architekten, Bern
1996–1999	Höhere Technische Lehranstalt (Ingenieurschule) HTL, Biel
2000–2002	Bart & Buchhofer Architekten, Biel
2003	AllesWirdGut Architekten, Wien
2004–2007	Jabornegg & Pálffy Architekten, Wien
2008	Salvi Renaudin Architekten, Bern-Wien
2009	Gründung von Schenker Salvi Weber ZT GmbH, Wien-Bern
2012–	Lehrauftrag TU Wien, Institut für Architektur und Entwerfen
2013	Mitglied des Schweizerischen Architektenvereins SIA
1974	Born in Bern
1990–1993	Draughtsman's apprenticeship at Schindler and Habegger Architects, Bern
1996–1999	Biel University of Applied Sciences
2000–2002	Bart & Buchhofer Architects, Biel
2003	AllesWirdGut Architects, Vienna
2004–2007	Jabornegg & Pálffy Architects, Vienna
2008	Salvi Renaudin Architekten, Bern-Vienna
2009	Founded Schenker Salvi Weber ZT GmbH, Vienna - Bern
2012–	Professor, TU Vienna, Institute for Architecture and Design
2013	Member of the Swiss Society of Engineers and Architects SIA

Thomas Weber

1970	geboren in Wangen
1991–1993	Tischlerlehre
1994–1998	HBC Hochschule Biberach
1999	Josef Prinz Architekt, Baindt
2000–2008	Dietrich|Untertrifaller Architekten, Bregenz-Wien
2005	Mitglied der Kammer der ArchitektInnen für Wien, Niederösterreich, Burgenland
2008–2009	Postgraduate an der Universität für angewandte Kunst, Wien
2009	Gründung von Schenker Salvi Weber ZT GmbH, Wien-Bern
2009–2013	Lehrauftrag TU Wien, Institut für Architektur und Entwerfen
1970	Born in Wangen
1991–1993	Carpenter's apprenticeship
1994–1998	HBC University Biberach
1999	Josef Prinz Architects, Baindt
2000–2008	Dietrich Untertrifaller Architects, Bregenz – Vienna
2005	Member of the Chamber for Civil Engineers and Architects for Vienna, Lower Austria and Burgenland
2008–2009	Postgraduate University for Applied Arts, Vienna
2009	Founded Schenker Salvi Weber ZT GmbH, Vienna – Bern
2009–2013	Professorship TU Vienna, Institute for Architecture and Design

MitarbeiterInnen / Collaborators

Otto Bäuerle, Sylvia Bonell, Stefan Dygruber, Christoph Frantes, Fatma Fistikci, Jarmila Fučíková, Matteo Furlan, Andreas Grasser, Falk Lennart Kremzow, Martin Maidl, Simona Masarova, Sven Mayer-Schwieger, Thomas Morgner, Slavomír Peterka, Hansjörg Reumann, Jakob Rockenschaub, Barbara Roller, Christian Rübenacker, Jana Sack, Adrian Schenker, Katharina Scheurich, Veronika Ševčíková, Pia Schmidt, Rostislav Stoklásek, Tina Tobisch, Katalin Tóth, Zsófia Varga, Philipp Wemmer

Ehemalige MitarbeiterInnen / Former employees

Tiago Santana, Tereza Tepla, Kristyna Trojanova, Teja Gorjup, Hannah Knittel, Peter Funke, Eva Andrasova, Maxime Aubry, Balthasar Freise, Marlies Grammanitsch, Andreea Suteu, Clemens Neuber, Bettina Doser, Teresa De Miguel, Alexandr Kulikov, Maria Luisa de Villalonga, Lennart Jansen, Rowena Ullrich, Sophie Gerg, Verena Theil, Christina Klonner, Alexandros Merkouris, Javier Cuenca Solana, Stefan Dobnig, Laure Finck, Merle Woköck, Carlos Guillermo De Simón-Altuna, Phoebe Stewart

Auszeichnungen / Awards	2013	Beispielhaftes Bauen Alb-Donau-Kreis und Ulm 2007–2013 (Haus S, Ehingen DE)
	2015	Yo.V.A. 4 Young Viennese Architects 4
	2017	Staatspreis Architektur und Nachhaltigkeit, Nominierung (Volksschule Absam Dorf)
		Office of the Year Award (Post am Rochus, Wien AT)
		best architects 16 award in Gold (Wohnbebauung Sillblock, Innsbruck AT)
	2018	AIT Award 2018 (Post am Rochus, Wien AT)
		best architects 19 award (Post am Rochus, Wien AT)
		Staatspreis Architektur und Nachhaltigkeit, Nominierung (Post am Rochus, Wien AT)
Ausstellungen / Exhibitions	2016/2017/2018	Alle wollen wohnen, Köln DE, Düsseldorf DE, Essen DE
	2018	JV-YoA 2018 Jogja Vienna-Young Architect Exhibition, Jogja Gallery, Yogyakarta, Indonesia
Vorträge / Lectures	2015	What's up?, AzW, Wien AT
		Creative Entrepreneurship, Universität für angewandte Kunst, Wien AT
		Fight Club, Mobiles Stadtlabor, Wien AT
		Zentralvereinigung der ArchitektInnen Österreichs, Bene Forum, Wien AT
	2016	Triflex Fachsymposium für Architekten und Planer, AzW, Wien AT
		AIT-Reise Office und Architektur, Andalusien
		Bauhaus-Universität Weimar AT
	2017	Pecha Kucha Night, Wien AT
		Hochschule für Technik und Architektur, Freiburg CH
		Architekturforum Bern CH
	2018	architektur in progress, Wien AT
		IoA Sliver Lecture Series, Universität für angewandte Kunst, Wien AT
		Turn On Architektur Festival, ORF Radio Kulturhaus
		Holzbauten, Bratislava SK
		Überbau Akademie, Wien AT
		Yo.V.A. Repräsentanten in Indonesien
		Architekturfestival Banja Luka
Bibliografie / Bibliography (Auswahl / Selection)		
Bücher / Books	2011	Kunst im öffentlichen Raum Niederösterreich. Band 10, Springer Wien-New York (Melktribüne Soundinstallation)
	2014	Bettina Rühm: Vorbildliche Grundrisse. Aktuelle Wohnhäuser für Singles, Paare und Familien, Deutsche Verlags-Anstalt (Haus S, Ehingen)
	2015	Tobias Schwarzer (Hrsg.): best architects 16 BOOK, zinnobergruen (Wohnbebauung Sillblock, Innsbruck)
		Grundrissfibel Schulbauten. 30 Architekturwettbewerbe in der Schweiz 2001–2015. Edition Hochparterre (Volksschule Kirchenfeld, Bern)
		Redaktionsbuero Architektur (Hrsg.): 100 deutsche Häuser – 2015/2016, (Haus S, Ehingen)
		Magistrat der Stadt Wien (Hrsg.): YoVA4. Junge Wiener Architekten und Landschaftsarchitekten, Young Viennese Architects and Landscape Architects
		Birkhäuser (Wohnbebauung Sillblock, Innsbruck; Volksschule Absam Dorf; Post am Rochus, Wien)
	2017	Ursula Kleefisch-Jobst, Peter Köddermann, Karen Jung (Hrsg.): Alle wollen wohnen. Gerecht. Sozial. Bezahlbar, jovis (Wohnbebauung Sillblock, Innsbruck)
Zeitungen/Magazine / Newspapers/Magazines	2011	Wohnbebauung Sillblock, Innsbruck. In: Architektur Aktuell Nr. 12
		Erweiterung St. Josef-Stiftung, Bremgarten. In: Hochparterre Wettbewerbe 4/Jahrgang 39
		Wohnüberbauung Brünnen, Bern. In: Hochparterre Wettbewerbe 2/Jahrgang 39
	2014	Wettbewerb als Entwicklungslabor, Interview mit Marta Schreieck und Michael Salvi. In: Architektur Aktuell Nr. 06

	2014	Post am Rochus, Wien. In: Architektur Aktuell Nr. 06
		Post am Rochus, Wien. In: Der Standard 14/05
		Wohnbebauung Sillblock, Innsbruck. In: Wettbewerbe Aktuell Nr. 01
	2015	Wettbewerbsstrategien. In: Der Standard 17/02
	2016	Post am Rochus, Wien. In: Architektur & Bau Forum Nr. 10
		Volksschule Bütze, Wolfurt. In: Architektur/Wettbewerbe, 40. Jahrgang, 325, Nr. 2
	2017	Volksschule Absam Dorf. In: Deutsche Bau Zeitschrift Nr. 11
		Post am Rochus, Wien. In: Die Presse 20/11
		Post am Rochus, Wien. In: Der Standard 11/11
		Post am Rochus, Wien. In: Home Nr. 09
		Volksschule Absam Dorf. In: Architektur Aktuell Nr. 05
		Volksschule Absam Dorf. In: Skin – Architektur & Bau Forum 28/04
		Volksschule Absam Dorf; Post am Rochus, Wien. In: Die Presse 22/04
		Post am Rochus, Wien. In: AIT – Architektur, Innenarchitektur, Technischer Ausbau Nr. 03
	2018	Bauen für Kinder (Volksschule Absam, Dorf). In: DETAIL inside Nr. 01
Dietmar Steiner (Textbeitrag / Article by)	1951	geboren in Wels Architekturstudium an der Akademie der bildenden Künste, Wien. Mitarbeiter von Friedrich Achleitner am «Architekturführer Österreich». Gründungsdirektor des Architekturzentrum Wien. Gastprofessuren in Harvard, am MIT, in Barcelona und Linz. Redakteur des Magazins «domus», Milano. Präsident von ICAM – International Confederation of Architecture Museums (–2014). Mitglied des advisory committees des «Mies van der Rohe Prize – Europäischer Preis für Architektur» und Mitglied der Jury des «european urban public space award» (–2016). Publizist und Architekturberater, jetzt Pensionist.
	1951	Born in Wels Studied Architecture at the Academy of Fine Arts Vienna. Employed by Friedrich Achleitner for the «Architekturführer Österreich». Founding Director of the Architekturzentrum Wien. Guest Professor at the MIT and in Harvard, Barcelona and Linz. Editor of the magazine «domus», Milan. President of ICAM – International Conference of Architecture Museums (until 2014). Advisory Committee Member of the Mies van der Rohe Prize – European Prize for Architecture, Jury Member of the «european urban public space award» (until 2016. Publisher and architectural consultant, now retired.

Finanzielle und ideelle Unterstützung / Financial and conceptual support

Ein besonderer Dank gilt den Sponsorfirmen, deren finanzielle Unterstützungen wesentlich zum Entstehen dieser Buchreihe beitragen.
Ihr kulturelles Engagement ermöglicht ein fruchtbares und freundschaftliches Zusammenwirken von Baukultur und Bauwirtschaft.

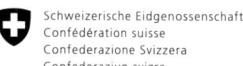

Schweizerische Eidgenossenschaft
Confédération suisse
Confederazione Svizzera
Confederaziun svizra

Eidgenössisches Departement des Innern EDI
Bundesamt für Kultur BAK

Arge Post am Rochus: ÖSTU-STETTIN Hoch- und Tiefbau GmbH, Wien

Arge Post am Rochus: HABAU Hoch- und Tiefbaugesellschaft m.b.H., Perg

Cascando Products b.v., Duiven (NL)

Tarkett Holding GmbH, Österreich

FCP Fritsch, Chiari & Partner ZT-GmbH, Wien, Berlin

Total Solution

Total Solution Architekturprodukte GmbH, Leibnitz

M.O.O.CON GmbH, Wien

Vitra Ges.m.b.H, Wien

Neudoerfler Office Systems GmbH, Neudörfl (an der Leitha)

ZG Lighting Austria GmbH, Wien

Quart Verlag Luzern / Quart Publishers Lucerne

De aedibus international
16 Schenker Salvi Weber – Wien (de/en)
15 Henley Halebrown – London (de/en)
14 Walter Angonese – Kaltern/Caldaro (de/en)
13 architecten de vylder vinck taillieu – Gent (de/en)
12 De Smet Vermeulen architecten – Gent (de/en, nl/fr)
11 Uwe Schröder – Bonn (de/en)
10 Stephen Taylor Architects – London (de/en)
9   Titus Bernhard Architekten – Augsburg (de/en)
8   Dietrich|Untertrifaller – Bregenz (de/en)
7   Geurst & Schulze Architecten – Den Haag (de/en)
6   Wingender Hovenier Architecten – Amsterdam (de/en)
5   Tony Fretton Architects – London (de/en)
4   Jonathan Woolf Architects – London (de/en)
3   Hufnagel Pütz Rafaelian – Berlin (de/en)
2   Hild und K - München (de/en)
1   Stanton Williams – London (de/en)

Monografien/Monographs
Peter Märkli – Everything one invents is true (en)
Emiliano López Mónica Rivera Arquitectos (de/en, sp/en)
koepflipartner – landschaftsarchitekten / landscape architects (de/en)
Graber & Steiger. Bauten und Projekte 1995–2015 (de)
Vincent Mangeat. Logos & Faber (de/en/fr)
Sergison Bates architects (de, en)
Peter Kunz. Bauten (de/en)
Miroslav Šik. Architektur 1988–2012 (de/en)
Valerio Olgiati (de, en)
Burkard Meyer. Konkret/Concrete (de/en)
Gion A. Caminada. Cul zuffel e l'aura dado (de/en)
Bearth & Deplazes. Konstrukte/Constructs (de/en)

Quart Verlag GmbH, Denkmalstrasse 2, CH-6006 Luzern;
books@quart.ch, www.quart.ch